THE QUAKE
YEAR

THE QUAKE YEAR

FIONA FARRELL

PHOTOGRAPHS BY
JULIET NICHOLAS

CANTERBURY UNIVERSITY PRESS

UNIVERSITY OF
CANTERBURY
Te Whare Wānanga o Waitaha
CHRISTCHURCH NEW ZEALAND

First published in 2012 by
CANTERBURY UNIVERSITY PRESS
University of Canterbury
Private Bag 4800, Christchurch
NEW ZEALAND
www.cup.canterbury.ac.nz

ISBN 978-1-927145-29-6

A catalogue record for this book is available from
the National Library of New Zealand.

Design and layout: Quentin Wilson, Christchurch
Printed by Everbest, China

Contents

Preface

There was life before the quake. And there is life after the quake. When you catch a glimpse of that previous Christchurch on video or film, it seems like history already. Another place, another time.

That jagged tear across a paddock at Greendale also ripped through people's lives, changing everything down to the smallest detail of everyday existence.

And it hasn't stopped. That is what the interviews in this book record: how it was before that early morning jolt altered everything, and how it was one year later, looking back as aftershocks continue their background rumble to the life of this city.

To begin with, this book was going to be very different. It was planned after the initial quake in September 2010, when it was assumed that the city had experienced The Big One and was safely on the road to reconstruction and recovery. The book was planned to have an element of celebration: we had survived!

February 22 changed all that and the ongoing tremors have left no room for complacency, let alone celebration.

Though in a way this book is a kind of celebration: of people's courage, resilience, kindness, creativity, generosity and sheer capacity for joy in the face of fear and loss. These stories are just a tiny sample: only 19, when there could be thousands, for everyone in Christchurch has their story of this shaken time. The sample, though, reflects the whole. Each story records a common experience, but it is in their individual responses that those qualities of courage, kindness and good humour are expressed.

The people whose stories appear here have been amazingly generous with their time and with their readiness to talk openly about painful experiences. It has been such a privilege to meet with them, to take photographs and to write down what they had to say.

Fiona Farrell
Juliet Nicholas

Tusiata Avia

'There were families with three kids, no car, no barbecue, no way of boiling water ...'

Finding Sepela: February 22

I am driving through the river/that is my road/to find my daughter/there are black sea creatures/eating white hippos/big as cars/I drive on the footpath/the drowning of wildebeests/whole herds of them in Breezes Road.

I get to the Aranui traffic lights and put my hand to my chest/I swear to her/drive with my hand on my heart/look into the dust cloud/blacken my eyes.

There are giant worms/under the ground/as big as Cairo/they eat the fish and chip shop/I promise her/her little ears/so far away/her heart/the sacred dome/the creamy marble/the white antelopes.

Five days go by/and still I drive/all on the roadside age/a woman pushes a pram/a cat peers out/a rabbit/a bird/I pass them/all women wear bare feet and walk/rhino/elephants/trains of them lie/in Philipstown/where they fall/it is catholic/this dream/it is total.

The house of the saints is not brick and mortar/but still it falls/everyone is leaving for their home/in the sky/Japanese/Chinese/Kiwis/and everyone/see them flying home/bright babies/through concrete steel and glass.

I promise my daughter/and run to Barbadoes/the holy sisters are fallen/look up through the broken window/god the mother has turned her back away/she looks down on us/she sends us blue and white.

My daughter is three/she shelters under the battle club/she hides inside the ground/the enemies of god/circle on the backs of buzzards/they rain bricks on the bus depot/the primary school/the preschool.

I snatch her up/like a football/I spring the slowest steps/it is underwater/this dream/it is eternal.

* * * * *

These are the words poet and performer Tusiata Avia wrote on the night of the

9

February 22 earthquake. That afternoon she had driven from the home she shares with her mother in Aranui across town to find her three-year-old daughter Sepela, who was at the Samoan Pre-school on Barbadoes Street. She first read the poem several weeks later at the Auckland Writers' and Readers' Festival in a session dedicated to Christchurch writers. I doubt that there was anyone in the room who was not moved to tears by her evocation of that nightmare sense of disbelief and dislocation.

But then Tusiata Avia's poetry often has that effect: tears, or laughter. She is a consummate performer, and a frequent guest at festivals throughout New Zealand and overseas. Audiences in Moscow, London, Rotterdam, Antwerp, Jerusalem, Bali, Morocco have applauded her as she shifts seamlessly from the voices of small children tormenting a dog called Bingo, to a 'bad girl'

tempting all the men as she walks through a village, to a poem about her uncle who acted as a double for Gary Cooper in that Hollywood version of a steamy island idyll, *Return to Paradise*.

On the page the words are compelling enough, but hear her speak those words, see her in performance and the impact is unforgettable. She has an extraordinarily powerful and compelling presence.

Today she is in mother mode. We have met to talk in a café in North Brighton. Sepela runs in and out from the outdoor play area, climbing onto Tusiata's lap for a cuddle before racing back to the rocking horse. Tusiata recalls the year in her thoughtful, unhurried fashion.

Of September 4 she says, 'I kind of think of that as my "Denial Earthquake". I just went into this state where I pretended it wasn't a big deal, even when I was lying

listening to everything smash. By the time the sun came up I'd taken this emotional position where I just didn't want it to be real. That was my way of coping. So when the power came back on and we could see what had happened in the city, I just wouldn't let it penetrate.'

A couple of days later she experienced a sudden flood of emotion in a supermarket carpark, a release of anxiety and anger that she firmly pushed aside. She carried on, caring for Sepela and working on her novel. She was that year's Ursula Bethell Writer in Residence at the University of Canterbury.

'Our house was okay: not much damage, just some crockery broken really. When there were aftershocks I just said, "No. Nothing's going to happen. It will stop." I didn't make any adjustments: didn't prepare an emergency kit or anything like that. My cousin who's a Mormon had always had an emergency kit – that's something Mormons do. They

have a big survival kit, with food and water. I think it's just for emergencies, but I used to think it was because of Armageddon and I always made fun of her. But I didn't prepare anything because doing that would have meant acknowledging that there was some danger, so I refused to go there.'

February was another matter entirely. When that quake hit she was working at her desk at home, sending emails. To begin with she simply sat – 'refusing to give in' as she puts it. She held on to her chair, until shelves pulled away from the walls and fell on top of her and she was thrown from side to side then forced onto the floor. She was also forced to acknowledge that in this event she was powerless.

'I remember lying there thinking, "Oh my god, I've got no choice here. I've got no choice what happens to me!" But even then I was also thinking that perhaps it was so overwhelming

because the epicentre was right under our house and that perhaps it wouldn't be so bad anywhere else. So even though I thought I should go and get Sepela from pre-school, I wasn't really worried for her.'

Tusiata's friend Hinemoana Baker rang from Wellington to ask if they were safe. Tusiata laughs in amazement, recalling that she replied with a calm and casual 'Oh yes, we're fine! We're fine!'

Out in the garage the car was buried beneath fallen things and for half an hour she had to sweep away broken glass before she was able to begin the drive into town. Turning onto Breezes Road she discovered the reality of the situation.

'Everything was under water: that whole area was flooded. Massive big holes had opened up and there were trucks, vans, half disappeared into these holes. And that was when it really penetrated. Then I got really,

really scared about what might have happened to Sepela.'

She recalled a sense of unease that morning when she had been driving Sepela past the Catholic cathedral on the way to drop her off at pre-school. The cathedral had received a little damage in September and was surrounded by a protective cordon of shipping containers.

'I was driving past and I thought, "If there's an earthquake today and that building falls down, I don't think those containers will be enough to protect people. People are going to get killed." It wasn't something I had ever thought before.'

She suppressed the feeling at the time, dismissing 'that little warning voice' as superstition. Now, she would not be so careless. She would pay attention to that little voice should she hear its caution again. That morning, however, she ignored it, and that

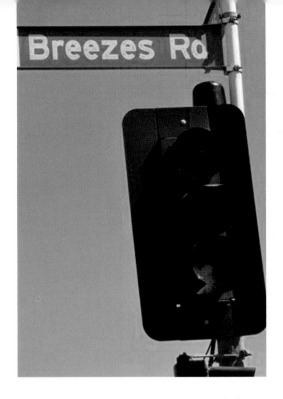

afternoon, driving down Breezes Road, she began to panic.

'I thought the whole of Christchurch must be under water because that was all I could see, and I thought, "How the hell am I going to get into town, when there's big holes in the road and I might disappear at any time? What am I going to do?" '

Although she was frightened, throughout she retained a certainty that Sepela was safe.

'I thought if she was dead I'd know.'

That certainty kept her going, driving slowly in heavy traffic as people fled from South Brighton, getting over the bridge leading to the city. Sometimes she drove on the road, sometimes on the footpath. The road was clogged with abandoned cars left by drivers who had given up and opted to walk. After two hours she finally reached Barbadoes Street, where she found Sepela, pale and frightened but unharmed, sitting out in the playground with the other children and their teachers.

'I felt so sorry for the teachers. Some of them had to wait till six o'clock before they could get away to check on their own families.'

The return journey took even longer, but by nightfall Tusiata and her little daughter were home again.

'There were so many people on the roads, walking. I put one of them in a poem: a woman pushing one of those old-fashioned prams with a cat in it, and a bird and a rabbit. She was just walking along the road.'

At home there was no power, no water, no sewerage. For a week they struggled on. Life was miserable and Tusiata felt terribly alone.

'It was awful. My cousin – we're very close – moved away to live with relatives in Bishopdale, and really, they might as well have moved to another city. It could take

'*My mum slipped over on the mud and hit her head. I just felt so responsible for everyone.*'

three hours to drive over there – the roads were treacherous. I felt isolated, like I'd been abandoned. And one night we went out for a walk to see how things were in the neighbourhood and my mum slipped over on the mud and hit her head. I just felt so responsible for everyone. It was tough.'

The other thing Tusiata found hard was the state of their whole neighbourhood.

'People were in a bad way. I mean, there were families on our street with three kids, no car, no barbecue, no way of boiling water, no way of getting to a shop if any were open and nothing in the cupboard except a packet of noodles. I got really indignant for people like them – the families who literally live week to week. We were watching the helicopters flying overhead and hearing on the radio that they were dropping off hot meals to people in South Brighton, but nothing was happening around here at all. Certain areas got a lot of

assistance. Some parts of Aranui had an active community and mobilised, like the area around the community centre on Hampshire Street, but in our little part of the world I couldn't see anything happening.

'Hinemoana was texting me from Wellington, saying, "Leave! Come up and stay with me! You can't live like that. It's not safe. You'll get sick!" And I knew she was right but I felt reluctant to leave. I don't know why. It was completely miserable. I hated it. Mum had gone into this World War II survival mode – making a big fire in the back yard to cook on et cetera – and I was so frustrated with her. I was saying, "Look, we can borrow a barbecue! One of the neighbours will have a barbecue! We can cook on that!" But she just refused. She wanted to do everything herself, which is typical of my mother. I didn't find out until later but she was actually rationing her food. She thought we'd have to stay there

14   THE QUAKE YEAR

for the duration. When I finally decided that Hinemoana was right and we had to go, it took a lot of convincing to get my mother to leave. I had to really bully her. I told her I wasn't going without her, so she could either come with me or go somewhere else, but she couldn't stay where she was.'

Finally her mother agreed to leave. Tusiata and Sepela went to Wellington for four weeks while her mother went to stay with Tusiata's brother, whose house in Burwood was still intact, and who had a generator. She stayed away until the basic services were restored to their street.

When they finally returned home Tusiata prepared an emergency kit and placed it in the kitchen, just in case. She also found the energy finally to write about what had happened. She wrote poems about visiting the inner city and the buildings that had been reduced to rubble. She also wrote an elegy for

a friend, Rhys Brookbanks, who died in the collapse of the CTV building.

Now she lives with deliberate quietness, trying not to add unnecessary stress to an already stressful year. She has learned to listen to herself, to the state of her body and her emotions, and she has learned not to ignore their signals. She has cut back on performance – though there is one she still hopes to fulfil.

In the New Year she has been invited

*She has learned to listen to herself, to
... her emotions, and she has learned
not to ignore their signals.*

to travel to England with the New Zealand
String Quartet and two other New Zealand
writers, Bill Manhire and Fleur Adcock,
to perform at Kings Place in London and
at StAnza, an international poetry festival
in Scotland. She will read the poem about
Rhys, the poem about the loss of the Samoan
church in the inner city, and the poem about
that nightmare drive through a strangely alien
environment into town to find her daughter,
who is at this very moment running in from
the café playground and climbing onto her
mother's knee.

I've been recording Tusiata's account on
a little digital recorder that lies on the table
between the coffee cups. Sepela is curious
about it. She wants to record something too.
So that is how this interview concludes: with
a little four-year-old singing very sweetly and
in perfect tune: 'Twinkle twinkle little star …
How I wonder what you are …'

St Paul's Trinity Pacific Church

No evidence
Of the backs of women's heads piled high with loops of hair
White hats pierced through like the side of Christ
No evidence
Of the train of ministers lining up all the way around the block
To their multi-storey home in the sky
No evidence
Of the baptisms, weddings and funerals of everyone we know
Of the gauzy clouds of White Sunday
Children hurtling out of the sky like hailstones
Shouting the words of the saints over and over
No evidence
Of the tiny pockets of air inside the mouths of women
The clicking of gums and the echoing of it up into the vaulted ceilings
Up into the ears of God
No evidence
Of the soprano, alto, bass
Of the men in their suit jackets and skirts
Bent and shuffling over the raspberry blood in sweet little glasses
Passing down through the 70s
Where they flapped to Engelbert and Tom in the church hall
No evidence
Of *Yellow Ree-vah, Yellow Ree-vah.*
You're in my mind and in my soul
No evidence
Of their straight backs in the 50s, their sharp suits
Their brylcreemed profiles handsome as movie extras
Returning us to Paradise.

We all fade into the archaeology
The Samoans, Cook Islanders, Niueans, Tokelauans
And Tongans of Cashel St and Madras.

We all snake forward to the tangled steel spaghetti
The spliced Corinthian columns
The disappeared gothic dome
The foolish man who built his house on the sand.

*...everything was down,
including a heavy iron
woodburner that had fallen
across their bed.*

Chris Moore

Chris is an elegant man as befits the arts editor of a daily newspaper: a man who has been known occasionally to sport a spotted bow tie. We meet in a bookshop in Riccarton. Before the February quake it was a shop specialising in technical books: men in anoraks silently scanned the shelves for information about German fighter planes, or manuals for the restoration of a 1966 Ford Cortina. Now it has a coffee machine and cakes on plates at the counter, the technical books have been joined by art and travel, and there are little tables filled with women and workers from the surrounding offices having lunch. Chat and the sound of the coffee machine punctuate our conversation.

In September last year Chris and his wife, Christchurch city councillor Claudia Reid, were preparing for the local body elections. September 4 was scheduled to be the first public meeting, with candidates gathered in the Gaiety Hall at Akaroa.

'That preoccupied us. Journalistically the end of the year in Canterbury is always busy.' There are features to write on the A&P Show and Cup Week. Not 'Fashion in the Field', he is quick to add, but a general 'My Big Day at the Show' sort of thing. 'They let the old Labrador out for the day.'

A sculpture festival, SCAPE, featuring pieces in outdoor spaces, required background articles and interviews with the various artists involved. The regular round of the arts page was a constant weekly presence. Life for Chris was 'pleasantly predictable'.

Each morning he caught the Lyttelton ferry from his home in Diamond Harbour, then the express bus into the city. The back of the bus was always occupied by the same familiar faces.

'We called it Club 28, after the bus. It

'Features was always a little tribe . . . slightly foppish. My bow tie confirmed the worst fears of the newsroom.'

was like a school bus for adults: an hilarious, wonderful experience. We'd all sit and talk about anything and everything on the outward journey and review the day on the return trip.'

Club 28 had a diverse membership: lawyers, journalists, council engineers – people who lived around the harbour basin but commuted to work in the city centre. Ever since Chris moved to Diamond Harbour 18 years ago he had been meeting up with the others on the 28 bus in this informal daily fashion.

The working day had other pleasant routines: lunchtime visits to Smiths secondhand bookshop 'to see Barry and buy something, much to the despair of my wife', or to Dafydd Williams in his little antique shop on New Regent Street.

'He was an old friend. He had a black spaniel, Cooper, who looked like Charles II. Cooper and I were great mates.'

The Press building itself had its character,

though in September 2010 things were planned to change. The paper was moving from its ornate Edwardian building in the Square to more modern quarters around the corner in Gloucester Street.

'I was on the second floor of the old building. From the reporters' room, they had built an extension out onto the roof to house the photographers, the library and – right at the end, as far as you could go – Features and Community Newspapers.'

Chris's desk originally had 'the most wonderful view of the cathedral spire launching itself above the roofs'. Unfortunately a new hotel had sprung up, blocking that view, and by 2011 Chris looked straight into a concrete wall.

It was nevertheless a 'nice place to work. I had all my bookshelves around me, all my books accumulated over 25 years of reviewing and trips to Smiths.'

He also had an old 1920s oak dining-room table donated by a former general manager where he could spread his papers. An office chair. A computer. Nearby sat the other features writers, 12 of them, and 15 or so subeditors, most of them people who had worked at the *Press* for a long time.

'Features was always a little tribe. No deadlines, slightly foppish. My bow tie confirmed the worst fears of the newsroom.'

Not that Chris had always written features. Back in 1963 he began work as an 18-year-old cadet on the *Nelson Evening Mail*, getting morning tea for the editor and chief reporter. (Effortlessly, he recalls exactly what they ordered: chelsea bun for the editor; cheese scone, lightly buttered, for the chief reporter; 'ghastly doughnut thing' for the chief sub.) There followed a stint of military service, a move to the *Otago Daily Times* in 1968, a spell in Wellington with Tourism and

Publicity, and then an appointment as press officer in the prime ministerial offices of Jack Marshall, Norman Kirk and Bill Rowling. In 1978 Chris returned to Nelson, met Claudia and moved with her to Christchurch, where in 1987 he took a job at the *Press*. He has been there ever since.

On the morning of September 4 he was sleeping restlessly.

'Claudia was nervous about the election meeting in Akaroa. Eventually I decided to sleep in the spare room. I remember walking through the sunroom about 4am and thinking how restless the birds were. It was still dark but I could hear the blackbirds chattering away and it seemed odd.'

He climbed into bed and the next thing he recalls is being woken abruptly by 'books falling on top of me. I became aware of this immense noise and swaying motion which became stronger till our little house seemed

to gyrate and slide.'

He scrambled through the dark and grabbed Claudia from the bed. Huddling beneath a doorframe he held her close against him, protecting her head lest something fall on her. They crouched in the doorway until the tremor stopped. Through the darkness they could see that everything was down, including a heavy iron woodburner that had fallen across their bed.

They groped their way through the clutter and debris as the aftershocks continued and – with some difficulty because the wardrobe door was jammed – they got dressed, fearing they might have to evacuate. They texted their daughter Hester, who was flatting in the city: she assured them she was fine. They became aware of neighbours moving about and found the sound of their voices reassuring. They decided to make a cup of tea, dashing into the garage to fetch a small gas cooker between tremors.

The mayor, Bob Parker, rang to check on the city councillor. As dawn broke she began moving between their home and the civil defence centre set up at the local fire station, while Chris tried to replace books and things that had fallen in their home. That week he was on leave from the *Press* but he went into the office the following day, working on reports of the quake from outlying places like Akaroa.

'It was strange, sitting at my desk. A woman in the adjoining office screamed loudly every time there was an aftershock – and there were a lot of them.'

The *Press* was advised to vacate the damaged building, so editorial staff moved – some to a city hotel and others out to offices in Logistics Drive, the *Press*'s Harewood printing plant. Eventually they returned to their old base in the Square, settling like so many

others to a slightly altered routine. Chris's morning bus followed a different route to the city. Within the city, buildings had been boarded up.

But no one had been killed.

'We had survived. There were no deaths. Canterbury stood up and dusted itself off. The *Press* put out a book titled *The Big One*. Claudia and I went to Sydney for a holiday. The earthquake almost faded from our minds.'

Except that on Boxing Day, as they were walking down to Sydney's Rushcutters Bay, Chris was overwhelmed by a feeling of total despair, a feeling he had never experienced before.

'Claudia asked, "Are you all right?" and I said no, not really. The feeling passed. A few hours later the Australian media reported a big aftershock in Christchurch. Frantic phone calls and texts home revealed that everyone

was shaken but all right. Hester was calm and matter of fact. Our house was undamaged.'

When they returned home they found business continuing more or less as usual. Claudia had been re-elected and was back into council work. Chris was back at the *Press*. The move to the new building was rescheduled for 4.30pm on February 25.

The days leading up to the move were filled with packing boxes and clearing desks. Chris was excited at the prospect of moving into his new office.

Our conversation pauses at this point. He has been talking animatedly, in his usual fashion, at the table in Edward Hooper Books. But now he slows: he has never really talked about that day to anyone other than Claudia until now.

'It was a curiously cold,' he says. 'A leaden summer day. I went early to lunch and then to the Salvation Army op shop. I always went

*'If we
thought
September
4 was bad,
this was
demonic.'*

on Tuesdays … one of my routines. I'm a magpie. That day I found an old Moody and Sankey Methodist hymn book. I was chuffed.'

He was back at his desk at 12.40. Colleagues were either returning from or leaving for lunch and the office was relatively empty when Chris decided he'd get a Coke from the cafeteria on the floor above. He found some change, stood up. And then it struck.

In the Press building in the centre of the city, directly over the fault-line, the force of the quake was astounding.

'If we thought September 4 was bad, this was demonic. It felt as if something simply wanted to kill you. It was intent on physically shaking us to death. As soon as it struck I dived under my desk. I think we all did. It was instinctual. Above the noise, I remember hearing a voice reciting the Rosary as the floor beneath me seemed to rise and fall. I felt

that we were suspended at times in mid-air. I thought, if this is death, I hope it's quick.'

The tremor lasted about 20 seconds but it seemed an eternity to the people clinging to shelter inside the heaving building.

'The noise was deafening but above it came this voice repeating "Hail Mary, full of grace …" '

Chris, strangely, was not frightened. Instead he felt complete peace.

'It was the most wonderful feeling: whatever happened, would happen. It was …' He pauses. He can't find the words at this moment. The coffee shop is all clatter and chat. 'And then,' he says, 'the shaking stopped. It went BANG. Like that.'

Then silence, broken only by the sound of the occasional falling object.

'What was truly frightening was the dense yellow dust cloud that cloaked everything. Gritty, dirty. It got into your eyes, your throat.'

Through a window Chris could see an external wall panel on the hotel next door slide downwards. People began to move around. Someone said 'I'm out of here!' and headed towards the stairs.

But Chris and a colleague, James Croot, were floor fire wardens. Suddenly they found themselves in charge of several dozen people. Chris asked everyone to stay exactly where they were while he checked out the evacuation route. He discovered that the exit was blocked by rubble and concrete from the third floor. Beyond the mass of twisted metal, brick and shattered wood lay the reporters' room.

'James suggested that we get out through the old printery at the back of the building. It was one of the oldest parts of the building, dark and confusing to anyone who didn't know it, but there was no panic. People who knew the building stood at intervals guiding and helping people. They were absolutely magnificent.'

Around them, the old building was disintegrating. ('Like a dog,' says Chris, 'shaking itself.') Unbeknown to Chris and his colleagues, people were trapped above them on the third floor. Someone had died. On the second level Al Nisbet, the *Press* cartoonist, was trapped beneath a fallen bookcase and ceiling tiles.

'You couldn't see him at all. But four of us managed to lift him clear.'

Photographer and ex-army man John Kirk Anderson led the small group in rescuing him.

'After heaving aside the debris we found Al curled in a foetal position, completely white, covered in dust. I thought he was dead but then he moved one arm.'

Nisbet, profoundly shocked and disorientated, was helped to his feet before, arms

CHRIS MOORE

around Chris, he was assisted down through the darkened, vibrating building to Press Lane. The entrance to Cathedral Square was complete blocked but they struggled under an archway and out into the relative safety of Gloucester Street.

'There were hundreds of people, but no panic. Half the *Press* staff were gathered there, but others, including the editor, Andrew Holden, were around the corner in the Square. So I volunteered to go and let Andrew know where we were.'

Turning into Colombo Street he saw that the spire of the cathedral had collapsed and its stately Victorian Gothic walls were in ruins. As he stood talking to Andrew there was another major aftershock and the tower at one corner of the Press building slid across the façade. Chris ducked down protectively, finding himself hugging the editor's secretary until the ground had stilled once more.

'Around us people were screaming and shouting directions. There was a badly tuned chorus of sirens. Dust everywhere. It really did feel as if the whole world was disintegrating.'

Andrew Holden indicated that *Press* staff should move away from the Square into Gloucester Street. Chris remembers meeting Peter Beck, dean of the Cathedral and an old friend, who told him there might be people trapped in the building. He also remembers an elderly lady, 'a little Canterbury lady, not a pearl out of place, a cathedral volunteer, 80-plus' who asked him to help her find a taxi.

'I asked if she was all right and she said, "Oh yes, dear, I'm fine." She'd hidden in the ladies' toilet during the quake but had been thrown around a bit and her hip was sore. She said, "I'm sorry to be a nuisance, but everything's such a mess. Do you think you could help me find a cab back to Fendalton?"

So I walked with her till I found someone who could look after her.'

Chris then set off to find Claudia, who had been at work in the council building. It had opened only a few weeks before, after extensive remodelling and renovation.

'I knew she'd be likely to have been at lunch at her regular coffee shop on Hereford Street, so I set off walking. No – not walking.' He corrects himself. 'Jogging. To find her.'

On the way he passed a fallen verandah. A man's legs protruded from beneath torn timber and corrugated iron. His shoes, Chris recalls with absolute clarity, were neatly polished. He passed buildings that swayed alarmingly in and out with each major aftershock. There was talk of people trapped in buildings and gas leaks. During one particularly vigorous aftershock in Victoria Square he lay flat on the ground, feeling it tremble beneath him and seeing 'about as close as that water carafe on this table' a little volcano bubbling up.

'I remember being mesmerised by this thing, and then it started spewing little gouts of grey water and I just lay there thinking, "This is bizarre. This is truly bizarre." '

At the council building he discovered that Claudia had been seen after the quake, alive and unharmed. He managed at last to make shaky phone contact: she was driving to their daughter's flat in Riccarton. At that point, separated from most of his colleagues, Chris decided to join the long lines of people walking towards Hagley Park.

'It was like some World War Two documentary of refugees trudging. That was the only word for it: we were *trudging*. The police kept saying, "Keep going. Hagley Park. Hagley Park." '

At the park, trees had toppled and the river was running like a sewer and a great

crowd of people had gathered, many in evident shock. Chris recalls an American woman, a delegate to an international United States–New Zealand conference, who plucked at his arm, endlessly saying, 'This doesn't happen in Washington … it doesn't happen in Washington.'

Another man obsessively demanded to know why there were no toilets or cups of tea. Teams of volunteers lugged heavy benches from the neighbouring bowling clubrooms to the rapidly filling space. Tents had been erected for the upcoming Ellerslie Flower Show and triage teams were able to move in. Chris found himself delegated, together with a young American from South Carolina, to meet and reassure hundreds of people as they arrived from the CBD. The American rose to the occasion with good humour, greeting people with 'Welcome, Ma'am, to Hotel Hagley. Can we be of assistance?'

'There were visitors who had lost their passports and airline tickets in hotels, people who were injured, whom we directed to the triage centres. And all the time Claudia was texting saying, "Where are you?" and I was replying that I was at the Ellerslie Flower Show site. But that made no sense at all to her. She'd forgotten all about the flower show. About 6 o'clock I looked up and there she was, walking towards me, indomitable and covered in dust.'

It was, he says, like a Hollywood reunion scene.

'I ran towards her in slow motion, and when I got to her she looked up at me and said, "Where the hell have you been? I've been looking for you for five sodding hours! And I kept getting these ridiculous messages – *I'm at the Ellerslie Flower Show!* What were you going on about?" And then she burst into tears.'

Together they drove home, taking a

'*It was like some . . . documentary of refugees trudging. The police kept saying, "Keep going. Hagley Park. Hagley Park."*'

long detour to reach Diamond Harbour where they found their house in a mess but relatively undamaged. Claudia told Chris about her experience of being tossed about the council rooms like a pingpong ball, getting badly bruised as the building swayed from side to side. (Despite the renovations it did not withstand the quake well and was abandoned for months while council staff worked from temporary premises.) With others she had then found her way down an unsteady staircase, before deciding to retrieve her car from the underground carpark: a very brave decision under the circumstances.

In the days following the destruction of its building, the *Press* was magnificent. An edition was on the stands the following morning, produced from Logistics Drive with the help of the *DominionPost* in Wellington.

'Our people were in a state of trauma, especially the staff from accounts and administration on the third floor who had witnessed injury and the death of a colleague. During the days that followed, journalists from around New Zealand and the world turned up. There were moments when I felt illogically angered by their presence. They were intruding on "our" trauma and grief. This was for them "just another disaster" – I had to go out and take a short walk from time to time.'

The *Press* administration took good care of its staff, checking on individual well-being, bringing in food. At 12.52pm a week later the entire staff met for a few moments' silence, holding hands in a circle, heads bowed as the jets took off from the airport nearby.

'That was a tough, emotionally charged moment,' said Chris. 'At the end Andrew Holden embraced me. I've never been hugged by an editor before in my life – had things thrown at me, but never a hug!'

Six months later he and the rest of

Holden's Heroes continue to be based at Logistics Drive, or, as it's called, Camp Fairfax.

It's cramped in the portacabins – 'terribly chummy', says Chris. 'Like a POW camp. Even down to football at lunchtime. In the early days we even took to whistling the theme from *The Great Escape*.'

Work starts early, at 7am, as the night staff with whom they share desks begin arriving early in the afternoon. It is, says Chris, about as far as it could possibly be from Club 28 and the bus into town and the office overlooking the Square with its view of the cathedral spire. It will be home for at least another six months.

He continues to edit the Arts pages and has edited and written a book of photographs and text by *Press* writers and photographers recording the February quake. There is no tempting fate this time with words like 'The Big One'. It is called simply *Earthquake*.

As we are ending this conversation among the coffee cups at Edward Hooper Technical Books I remind Chris that this is the second time I have heard of him responding to the imminence of death. Some years ago the ferry to Diamond Harbour was in collision with another boat. Fearing the ferry was about to go under, a mutual friend had dived into the water, and found herself being dragged back toward the propeller. Chris had, with great presence of mind, reached over and held her clear of the blades. At those times, he says, you know in a split-second that you have two options: one is to give in and the other is to say, no, sorry, it's not time yet.

And it's only then that he tells me that somewhere – he still has no memory of exactly where – between the Press building and Hagley Park, shortly after he had seen those sad polished shoes, he had passed a car. There was a man trapped inside by fallen

masonry. He appeared unconscious as Chris and another man forced the car door open.

'He fell out into my arms,' says Chris. 'Then he looked up and died. There was no blood or obvious signs of injury. We carried him to a clear space and laid him on a tarpaulin and a young policeman told us there was nothing we could do. "Leave it to us, mate," he said.

'It was a gentle death, if you can describe death in that way. For a couple of weeks afterwards I became obsessed with trying to find out where it had happened, who it was, until one of my colleagues noticed my obsessiveness and said, "Chris, you must stop doing this. You have to accept that you did the best you could. And it's better he died in someone's arms, rather than alone." So: I've left it there.'

But the memory is clearly deeply painful. Chris often thinks of that man he doesn't know in that place he can't quite remember.

And then, just as we are rising to go, he reaches into his pocket.

He visited Padua a few years ago. And isn't it the most beautiful little city? He and Claudia had gone to see the great pilgrimage church of St Anthony. Waiting for Claudia in the cloister he had met an Australian-born Franciscan friar.

'We had a short but wonderful conversation, sitting in the sun and talking beneath the Gothic arches, the way you sometimes do when you meet strangers when you travel. And when he left, he gave me this,' says Chris. He pulls a rosary from his pocket. A plain humble wooden rosary worn by Franciscan brothers.

It was in his pocket on February 22.

If Chris has a memory of February 22, it is this: crouching in the shadow of death while around him the familiar world shook to pieces, all the while feeling the beads, smooth, warm and comforting in his hand.

'Christchurch is my home. I'm not planning to move.'
Karen Duncan

I talk to Karen Duncan on her day off. She shows me her work schedule: five morning shifts, two days off, four afternoon shifts, two days off, three morning shifts, two days off, three afternoon shifts, one day off, four morning shifts, one day off … It looks complicated, but she rattles it off effortlessly. She has been a nurse 'on and off' since she was 18 and is well used to the intricacies of hospital timetables.

Karen works in the operating theatres at Christchurch Public Hospital: paediatrics in the mornings, mostly orthopaedics in the afternoons and weekends. It was not always her choice to be a nurse: she studied English and fine arts at university and retains a strong interest in fiction. When she is not at work, she is at the gym, or taking photographs, or at her home in St Albans in a house she loves for its perfect 1950s detailing, writing a novel. It's about people dealing with the consequences of tragedy.

Most of her working life has been spent in this city. Born in Reefton, she was brought here when she was three. Mother, sister and other family members live nearby and it was at Christchurch Public that she trained before heading off overseas for some extended travel.

'I wanted to do something practical, and something that would take me out into the big wide world. In fact I didn't nurse much. I worked on a farm in the States and then in Chicago as a waitress – though nursing did come in handy there. I remember a kids' birthday party where one of the kids vomited. I just cleaned it up without thinking about it. The other waitresses were all these expensive Ivy League college girls and they were "How could you DO that? How could you BEAR that?" I didn't know what they were talking about. The mother was so apologetic and I got a HUGE tip.'

For a year she was an au pair in Paris, then in England she returned to nursing, working in surgical wards. She has always preferred surgical to medical work, and theatre work above all.

'Theatre work is very practical. It's physical, as well as being mentally challenging. You're working with the surgeons, setting up machinery.'

Is it like it is on the telly? I ask, since *Grey's Anatomy* is the closest I get to an operating theatre.

'It's a lot calmer,' she says. 'And the anaesthetist always gets ignored on TV. They're much more part of things in real life. When I see one of those programmes I always look to see what instruments have been laid out. More often than not they've got instruments on the table that have no relation to the surgery they're performing. There was a movie on Friday night that anyone with

medical training could not bear to watch: it was supposed to be neurosurgery for head trauma and they hadn't even intubated, that sort of stuff. I don't watch medical programmes much. Too close to work.'

Karen loves the physicality of her job. 'You're standing, moving around a lot, there's a lot of lifting.' She keeps fit with regular trips to the gym and swimming, and she usually cycles to work.

On September 4, a Saturday, she was scheduled for a morning shift.

'On a morning shift I work in paediatrics. Evenings and weekends we run three acute theatres, and while every speciality is covered, the bulk of the works falls into three categories: orthopaedics, general surgery and plastic surgery – often lacerations, tendon or nerve repairs. Normally I work in orthopaedics.' The number of cases in a single shift varies depending on need: sometimes several,

sometimes a single major op. 'We just keep rolling through.'

That morning, when her house began shaking and a shoe rack toppled onto her bed and there was the sound of things falling in the kitchen, Karen's first thought was, 'This is BIG. There are going to be casualties.' She got her landline phone and her cellphone and placed them both by the bed.

'I could see the neighbours were walking round outside with a flashlight but I didn't want to go out myself. I knew that at the least we'd be very busy next day and I'd have to be able to function, so my priority – if I wasn't called in sooner – was to get as much sleep as I could. Except I kept thinking about those glass cases at Pompeii with all those people buried in ashes mid-crawl, and I was think- ing, "Just relax! If I'm going to end up being put in a glass case by some archaeologist, I want to look relaxed! I want to be nicely

mounted!" (At this point the recording explodes into laughter. You laugh a lot when talking to Karen.) 'I suppose I thought this might be it, the end. But not directly. You acknowledge it in a kind of oblique way.'

Before she went back to bed Karen had texted family. She had also checked on a dog she was looking after for a friend. 'I heard her yelping in the laundry and found her under a pile of stuff from the shelves. I was scared that she'd run off if I opened the back door so I let her out to run around the house a bit and she peed on my carpet. And I thought, "Fair enough! I feel like doing that myself!" '

She avoided checking for damage throughout the house, but she could see that the kitchen was a mess of broken bottles of vinegar and assorted sauces. She cleared what she could, then rinsed her feet and went back to bed 'smelling like a Chinese takeaway'.

'It was funny at work that day: everyone

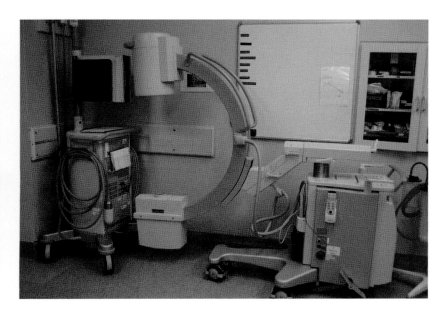

was saying, "Balsamic vinegar! Soy sauce!" '

That morning she drove to work anticipating the worst.

'I was looking out the window expecting to see fallen trees, and when I didn't see any obvious damage I thought it couldn't be too bad. The most difficult thing was driving through intersections with no lights working. I didn't notice the fallen chimneys. I was so concerned with what I might be confronted with when I got to work that I didn't even notice the shops that had collapsed at the corner of Westminster and Cranford Street. Didn't see them at all.'

When she arrived at the hospital at 8am the co-ordinator was discussing with medical staff which cases took priority for the morning. Theatres were checked. Many of the theatre beds and heavy equipment, although braked, had moved. Stock had fallen from shelves.

'The electricity had been off at home, so I'd been thinking I'd be able to grab a cup of tea at work. But the power supplied from the generator didn't extend to the urn in the tearoom.' However, someone managed to find a jug and boiled up quietly in a corner. 'I got half a cup from that. I was allocated to the orthopaedic theatre and we spent the day with a person who had suffered multiple trauma.'

As she worked, Karen found herself suffering from motion sickness.

'There were aftershocks the whole time and I had to concentrate on the equipment, find the correct screws for the plate we'd inserted, check each one for the correct length with everything moving underneath me. It made me feel quite sick.'

Work over, she drove to her sister's for tea. Their house had been more badly damaged (six months later in the February quake it

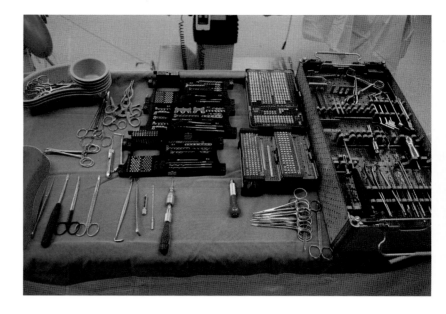

'*A whole lot of screws in the sets I had open on my table jumped out of their slots.*'

was to be condemned) but 'we all hugged each other, got a bit teary, spoke to family in Wellington. I felt a bit shaky, but the thing that really surprised me was that we hadn't had more casualties. We had been really fortunate.'

In the months that followed, Karen's daily routine altered a little. The Centennial gym she normally attended had to be closed, so she moved across the city to Jellie Park for her exercise. But generally after that first rather shaky day, life settled down. Karen worked, wrote her novel, spent time with family and friends.

On Tuesday February 22 she was at work. She was planning her 50th birthday party for the following Saturday – 'the first time I've ever been so organised in my entire life'. Family were coming from Wellington and Auckland, food and drink had been ordered.

'At midday I was scrubbed up for an

orthopaedic operation when I felt the whole room tip. It tipped one way, then it tipped the other way. There was this big X-ray machine, about two metres square, with screens and a C-arm: they take X-rays during orthopaedic operations to check the fracture is reduced, plates are positioned correctly and that screws are correctly positioned and the correct length. It's big but it moved – just like one of those pens with a little boat in it that shifts when you tip the pen. It just sailed across the room in one direction then sailed back the other way, as if it was floating.'

The theatre staff's greatest concern was that their patient remained safe, but 'while we were holding on to him, a whole lot of screws in the sets I had open on my table jumped out of their slots. The diameters of the screws are specific to each set and within the set they're laid out so you can see the diameter and length of the screw, but when

they jumped out everything was in a muddle. The lights flicked off, then the generator kicked in but it's not the light you're used to working with under normal conditions. One of the anaesthetists said, "We're going to have casualties from that!" There were two of them in the room, so he went downstairs to see what was happening in Emergency while we continued with the operation. When he came back he said casualties were already coming in. Nobody said much. We just carried on without talking.'

On and off throughout the afternoon the generator stalled and 'we were told we only had so long of battery power but then the generator would kick in again. The maintenance people must have been down there, working like beavers.'

She didn't think about such things at the time. 'The good thing about being scrubbed is you're just totally focused on what you're

doing. You're aware of what else is happening around you, but your energy is totally on the job on hand.'

Recalling that afternoon six months later is a bit of a blur. There was a brief interval while incoming patients were examined in Emergency. During this break Karen unscrubbed and was able to go to her locker for her cellphone to check on her family. The change room was in complete darkness. A friend had just got out of the shower.

'She had no idea where her locker was. It was quite disorienting. Then someone came in with a cellphone and with the light from its screen we managed to find her locker and then mine. I had a text from my sister in Auckland asking if I was all right. She said she had contacted my mother and sister and they were fine.'

By the time Karen returned to theatre it had been cleaned and set up and the first

'One of the anaesthetists said, "We're going to have casualties from that!"'

person from the quake was being wheeled in. Surgeons had arrived over from Burwood to help. Karen stayed in the orthopaedic theatre. Other theatres had also taken quake cases. One of the managers organised for some staff to go home and come back for a night shift so they could keep theatres operational into the night.

'No one had much idea of what it was like outside. When the afternoon shift came in at 3 o'clock one girl said her bedroom window had smashed so I assumed my house would be a wreck. And someone mentioned the cathedrals had come down and that cars were parked anywhere and everywhere on the road.

But Karen just kept herself focused on what was happening in theatre. She worked till 6 o'clock, then cycled home to sleep, ready for the next day. It was hard. She had witnessed young people coming into theatre

badly hurt. Amputations are often of old or necrotised flesh, but these people were young and healthy and their lives were going to be totally altered. She felt deeply shocked. Big blocks of that day have vanished from her memory.

'I do remember when I went to go home I couldn't walk the route I normally take to the bike stand, so I made my way to the lower ground floor, which was a big mistake. It's an impersonal labyrinth of corridors in the best lighting conditions, but in pitch black with water all over the floor it was creepy. I thought, "If I get lost down here, no one would find me for weeks."'

She got outside finally and cycled home. In September there had been people out on the streets, surveying the damage. On the evening of the 22nd there was no one. Karen cycled across Hagley Park cycleway through puddles of liquefaction and along the

near-deserted streets to find her house intact, windows unbroken, more sauce and china on the floor and no power or water to clean it up. A friend arrived with a flask of coffee and potato chips.

'That was lovely, sitting on the floor eating potato chips. Then he took me back to his house in Burnside. He still had power on and not too much damage. On the way we stopped off at my mother's. She was already in bed and shocked but okay. My sister and brother-in-law had had to leave their house, so they were staying in one of the spare rooms.'

Next morning she returned to work to find that more staff from Burwood had arrived with extra equipment. That whole next week the operating theatres at Christchurch Public Hospital were full, with staff performing a huge number of orthopaedic operations. Each night when her shift ended,

Karen cycled home through the strange city.

'The area around the hospital had been cordoned off. There was no one around, just some army guys. One night I cycled over the bridge past that statue of Rolleston. It had fallen over and I thought, "He's got a really bad head injury!" The back of his skull was smashed and his neck was broken. I wondered about taking a photo and normally I would have done, but I didn't have the heart for it.'

Six months later, sitting in her 1950s kitchen with a fresh ginger cake lending an authentic 1950s scent to the room, Karen feels more optimistic.

'I feel sad about the city, but quite pragmatic really. I miss things like that beautiful old brick building near the library with all its little archways. It's devastating in a way – but it's also going to be interesting to see what they do, how they rebuild it.

'*So much of life is just dealing with what you're given.*'

Anyway, Christchurch is my home. I'm not planning to move.'

Karen will continue cycling to work at Christchurch Public, go to the gym, see friends, write her novel.

'The quake's had some effect on my writing. The book is about a group of characters who were involved in a tragic event for which one of them was blamed, and about how they come together much later and how that event has affected them. I was struggling with the end but the quake clarified things for me. I realised how quickly things can be taken out of our hands. So much of life is just dealing with what you're given. We don't have total control over our lives.'

The nature of her job reinforces this awareness.

'One thing about my work is that you're aware life can change in an instant. You see people who have suffered accidents come up in their work clothes and you realise they were just going about their daily business and suddenly they've experienced an event that has changed their life.

'I think the quake has made us all more aware of that. We think of luck as a kind of extra, but really we're just fortunate to get away with things. I think people were more aware of that in the past: people died from diseases, people died or were disfigured from accidents – but we'd largely forgotten that. We'd forgotten about our vulnerability to huge events.

'That's what this year has forced us to remember.'

The car tipped over the edge of the road. Sam braked but it didn't seem to make any difference. They were crashing through the bush. Sam's knuckles were white as they gripped the steering wheel. Foliage flicked over the windshield. He could smell it – bleeding trees. Finally something hit the bottom and they came to an abrupt stop. Sam's body, pushed back by the sudden descent, lurched forward and his chest hit the steering wheel with a thud. The radio was playing. It hadn't been on before but something had jolted it into action. Sam listened to a string of advertisements, too frightened to look at his son. When he turned it was to see Liam struggling with his seatbelt. He leant over and unlatched it for him.

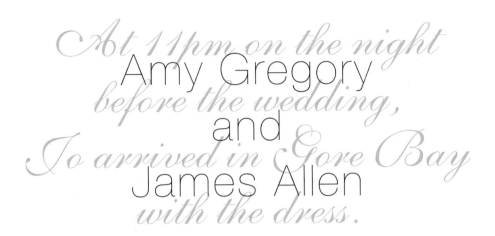

Amy Gregory
and
James Allen

At 11pm on the night before the wedding, Jo arrived in Gore Bay with the dress.

I talk with Amy Gregory and her husband James Allen in their house in South Brighton. It's cosy and sunlit, a first home for the couple who are expecting a baby in three weeks' time. The kitchen is its original vivid 1960s blue and the living-room walls are decorated with collectable skateboards. James is a sales rep for a snowboard manufacturer and is a keen skateboarder. The long expanse of Brighton Beach lies only a block away, the sound of waves audible – though right now the road is busy with heavy machinery replacing sewer-age pipes. Orange cones and diversions make a maze of getting there and I'm a bit late, but Amy's mother Ann has made afghans, her father David is visiting after work, and James arrives at the same time as me, back from a day snowboarding at Mt Hutt.

Amy and James bought the house in September, just before the first quake. They had settled that very week – a hugely exciting moment, after looking for over a year while living in a downstairs room in David and Ann's house on a hillside at Governors Bay. But when they were only days from moving into their new home in Brighton, the ground erupted beneath their feet.

'It was really reassuring being at Mum and Dad's,' says Amy, even though it had seemed at first as if the house might slide down the hill. When the shaking ceased, they called to one another in the dark, and all were safe. 'Then Dad swung into full GI survival mode, with a windup torch, radio and instructions for us all.'

Meanwhile, James filled the bath, after ringing his parents who lived in Avonside.

'That would definitely be the first time they've ever heard from me at 4.30am!' he says. They too were unharmed. Their house was another matter: from that day on, for an

entire year, his parents have been able to live only in the downstairs rooms.

No one had been injured. 'We drove to Brighton to check our new place. On the drive over, once we were through the tunnel, we could see the extent of the damage across the city.'

Their new home, luckily, was unharmed, but the move to Brighton immediately became more problematic. Suddenly no insurance company was willing to cover their house – and without insurance, the bank was no longer prepared to lend them money.

'There were a couple of hundred other buyers in Christchurch caught like us that day, including someone at my work,' Amy says. 'I spent that next week on the phone trying to organise it, before the media heard about it all through Jacqui, my sister-in-law who worked for a law firm. I did an interview on *Checkpoint* and it still took weeks of

*A hundred aftershocks, 1000, 1500
— until no one bothered
counting any longer.*

to-ing and fro-ing before the vendor's lawyer managed to arrange a transfer of insurance.'

Finally, in late October, Amy and James were able to move in, and over the next few weeks everyone settled to adaptation to this strangely shaky new world. A hundred aftershocks, 1000, 1500 – until no one bothered counting any longer.

They went ahead with plans for their wedding: a 'Beach Party Celebration' they had planned for March 5, 2011 at Gore Bay near Cheviot. Invitations were sent out to friends in Glasgow, China, America, Australia and all around New Zealand. Amy and James booked out the Gore Bay campground. James worked on his '65 Chevy Impala to transport the wedding party, and Amy began searching for the perfect wedding dress. For a long time she had no success.

'I was beginning to think I would never find a dress in Christchurch but one day I happened to pop into an antique shop. They only had one wedding dress in the whole shop. The owner went out the back to get it – and I loved it! It was 1950s, grosgrain, made in Timaru, and still in its original box. It needed some alterations to fit properly, but I asked a friend of mine who is a designer, to alter it.'

That friend, Kathryn Leah Payne, is well known for her exquisite clothing and accessories. Her studio was on the sixth floor of a building in the Square, just opposite the cathedral. She was at work on Amy's dress, in fact, on February 22 when another fault-line fractured beneath the central city, demolishing the cathedral in a matter of seconds and destroying buildings throughout the CBD, including her studio. Kathryn managed to escape, fleeing down dark and shaky stairs. But everything was left behind on the sixth floor: her computer, her bag, her patterns, her

AMY GREGORY AND JAMES ALLEN   45

'My sister was on the 10th floor of Clarendon Towers for three hours until she was rescued by firefighters . . .'

machines, and of course Amy's dress.

Amy was at a client's home, discussing therapy for a child afflicted with encopresis.

'We were talking about making a game of it – how to defeat "Sneaky Poo" – when the room began to shake. After it stopped I just carried on with the session. I felt scared, but I thought it was just a really strong aftershock. I got a text from James: Are you ok? It wasn't until I was back in the car and heard the radio that I started worrying about family and friends.'

James was across the city at the snowboard company's office in Bromley after a morning visiting stores in the city centre.

'I was heating up leftovers for lunch when BAM! We were on the second floor of a concrete slab building, me and two work-mates, when everything started shaking. We couldn't walk; I grabbed the doorframe and them in between my arms. When it stopped we went outside. I let the puppy in the office off the lead and then the second shock came. The asphalt wobbled like waves and when I looked down the cul de sac there was another building – same design as ours – and the front had just fallen off it. The road was slumping, the sewers were breaking through, and then everything went crazy. The whole place filled with boy-racers getting out. They were flooring it, drifting, going down the street sideways in their cars like it was Friday night.'

James was relieved to hear back from Amy but was worried about his mother, living in her kitchen in her damaged home on Avon-side Drive. He set off to drive there but the roads around Bromley were filling fast with liquefaction, and cars and trucks were getting stuck in sink-holes. He decided to head home to Brighton instead, but that too proved impossible: a bridge was out, and the road was deep in water and sewage. He abandoned

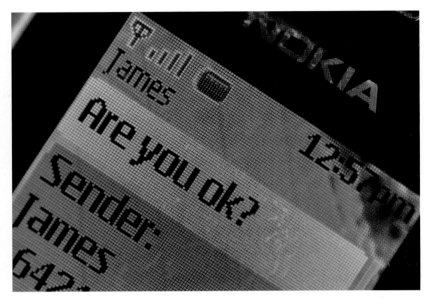

his car and set off toward the city on foot, though he took the precaution of first removing his shoes. 'They were brand new. I didn't want them to be completely ruined.' In bare feet he walked west until he met a friend who had a couple of mountainbikes.

'She didn't want to be left alone at her place so we biked to Mum's down Breezes Road, through water the whole way. On Avonside Drive there were waterfalls into the river, and there was this Māori warden whose son was on the other side and he'd swum across to get him. Mum was home. My sister had sent a text: she was on the 10th floor of Clarendon Towers for three hours until she was rescued by firefighters, and my Dad was ferrying people on Avonside Drive to their homes in his 4WD.'

Amy meanwhile was caught in the traffic that had instantly jammed the city's streets. She was feeling nauseous. Only a week earlier she had discovered that she was in the early stages of pregnancy.

'It was a work car and I had no food or water apart from a bag of nuts. It took three hours to drive back to work and I got more and more stressed about my family and friends.'

The aftershocks alarmed her, as did the worsening reports on her car radio, confirming that people had died. It was impossible to get through on the phone to anyone in Christchurch but Amy did manage to speak to her sister, Lucy, in Wellington.

'I kept crying to her. We still didn't know if Mum and Dad were okay. When I got back to work I left the car and decided to walk, rather than face getting stuck in more traffic in my own car. I was going to go and see a friend who I thought might be on her own with a baby, but on the way I stumbled across her partner, so we all walked to James's

parents' place in Avonside. His brother and sisters turned up there too, and that's where we all stayed for the next two nights. James and I didn't want to be in Brighton. We wanted to stay with family and friends: it felt really important to stay together in one house, even if it was damaged and there was no power and the water and sewerage were out. We wee-ed in the garden and we watched TV in James's brother's BMW. It's got a little TV. We all crammed into the car with this six-inch screen. That's how we could see what was happening to our city. We got water from a truck that had driven over from Rangiora. We collected it in bottles and we cooked everything on the barbecue.'

Amy's parents had also crossed the city and got home to Governors Bay. David works for Environment Canterbury in a tower that had been earthquake-proofed in the '90s with rubber insulation.

'It flexed like a fishing rod and everything fell over. I got downstairs – four flights with bits of concrete falling – and out into this dusty fog. I hadn't used my usual parking place that day and the car that was there had been completely squashed. The boss said to us, "Go home and find your family!" So I just focused on doing that. I drove down the central median strips on Brougham Street, and along the railway line between a couple of city blocks. I followed a campervan that simply nose-dived into a great hole in the road over near Heathcote: the doors opened and the people scrambled out and sploshed to the sides.'

When David reached home, it was to find that a window had exploded. Ann wasn't there. She is a resource teacher working with children who are visually impaired. Together with other teachers, she was waiting with the children lined up outside on the playground

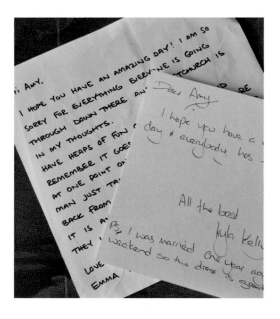

Amy's sister Lucy had put a message out on Facebook: 'My sister's dress is trapped!'

at Elmwood School in Merivale while parents gradually came in from all over the city to collect their sons and daughters. She remembers every detail of the journey home and the surreal feeling of hearing helicopters and ambulances and seeing groups of people crying. David said that seeing her arrive home at last was 'like one of those running-along-the-beach movie scenes'.

A week and a half after that horrendous day, Amy and James got married.

'We didn't really contemplate cancelling the wedding,' says Amy. 'It felt right to have a celebration with all the people we love. Most of our friends were insistent about being there. Even those from overseas wanted to be with us and be a part of something positive.'

Of course the preparations had changed completely. The wedding dress, for example – the beautiful antique gown from Timaru – was trapped in Kathryn's studio in the wreckage of the Square. Amy was gutted. But it felt insignificant; people had died.

'Stressing about my lack of wedding dress was minor.'

Up in Wellington, however, Amy's sister Lucy had put a message out on Facebook: 'My sister's dress is trapped!'

'She gave my size, and suddenly all these people began offering me their wedding dresses. Then my friend Dene contacted 91ZM who interviewed me, and there were dozens of emails: "She can borrow my dress!" A courier company said they'd cover the cost of delivery. When Dad went into a bakery to pick up the bread for the wedding the woman behind the counter said, "Wait a minute! I've got a dress at home. I'll just run and get it!" There were all these dresses arriving and people had put little cards in wishing us well. We've kept all the cards. I was blown away, it meant so much that complete strangers were

offering their special dresses to me.'

Then two days before the wedding, after Amy and James had left to set up the site for the wedding at Gore Bay, James's friend Jo, who works for Newstalk ZB in Christchurch, decided to act: she would try to get the original dress out of the studio in the Square. The buildings were completely off limits, the area in chaos, but Jo persisted, phoning Civil Defence until she was able to lodge a request for a USAR team, then waiting at headquarters for hours until there was a brief gap in the mass of urgent requests. A small team of USAR experts and engineers accompanied her to the Square. Kathryn had supplied detailed directions. A couple of engineers sprinted up six flights through the ruined building and at 11pm on the night before the wedding, Jo arrived in Gore Bay with the dress. Despite being unable to access her own samples, patterns, machines and

materials, which remained beyond recovery in the wreckage of her studio for another three months, Kathryn had the generosity of heart to complete the alterations to Amy's dress. It fitted perfectly.

So Amy and James had their wedding. Friends and family gathered from far and near at Gore Bay. They camped by the beach. On Saturday, the sun shone for the ceremony. James's precious Impala wasn't able to be finished in time, so a motorbike brought him to the beach. David read a poem he had written especially for the occasion. And Amy wore the grosgrain dress.

Afterwards they had a barbecue dinner. People had made salads, and a community group in Cheviot pitched in, producing chocolate cakes, cupcakes and 'beautiful lemon cakes' in return for a $200 donation to the Earthquake Fund.

'It was such a joyous occasion, a real

community wedding. We hadn't seen a lot of our friends since the earthquake and the day had an overwhelming feeling of joy and poignancy. Friends had lost their homes and businesses and been through scary experiences. James and I felt so grateful they were all there to share the day with us. And the dress was part of all that. I kept looking down at it and smiling, thinking of all the people who had made it possible for me to wear it. It was just awesome.'

And now, in their home at Brighton, Amy and James excitedly await the birth of their baby. This week, James's work has shifted to safer ground in Wanaka, but Amy and James plan to stay here. They plan a home birth, here in their home in Brighton. They plan to stay in this city, among family and friends.

Because to them, that is what matters most.

This Place of Meeting
(for Amy and James)

This is the place of meeting
– the sea, the land –
the sky as witness.
Each day the same
and each day changing.
Each day, the sun, the tide
reveals a beach
that no one has walked before,
the sand smoothed,
ready for your footprints.
This beach is yours,
to walk together.
May it ever be,
sea-smoothed,
waiting for you.

– David Gregory

Robert walked out into sewage and liquefaction up to his knees.

Lyn Fossey

Two ebullient dogs greet me at the gate: a big black Labrador called Buster and a six-week-old curly-coat with a tight brown fingerwave and amber eyes who is called Bear. Lyn wanted to call him Choccydoodah but her husband put his foot down. The dogs tussle while Lyn and I settle to talk on the deck at the back of the new cottage she and Robert have bought at Pines Beach, a short distance from their former home at Kairaki Beach, north of Christchurch at the mouth of the Waimakariri River. The new house is snug and already comfortably furnished, though Lyn and Robert moved in only five days previously. She has taken a day's leave from her job in a jewellery shop in Rangiora to finish unpacking. The yard already has its garden borders, with new plants tucked in for spring. There is a large run across the back fence for Buster and Bear and a bench in a shade-house in the most sheltered corner for warm summer days. There is a shed for Lyn's chickens. In the middle of the lawn stands an old clawfoot bath that contains 11 goldfish. They flick about, patchy orange and white, under pondweed. A space next to the house has been cleared for a large canvas gazebo, which lies in pieces on the lawn ready for Robert to install when he returns from work in Christchurch. It will provide shelter for an outdoor table. It's three months out, but Lyn is already planning Christmas dinner with the whole extended family.

Lyn fetches iced tea and we sit in the sun, talking while the dogs scuffle on the lawn like a couple of rumbustious teenagers. Some-times they race past, their tails threatening to knock everything from the low table, and Lyn growls. They slow down temporarily and slink off looking guilty.

The air is sweet here near the coast with

the scent of lupin and the pine trees that form a backdrop to the house and cover the sand dunes between this little settlement of Pines Beach and the wild sweep of coastline that borders Pegasus Bay. There is a gate in the back fence leading to the network of sand tracks that traverse the plantation, where people like Lyn and Robert can walk their dogs the half-kilometre down to the sea. Wild plum trees have taken root here, and on this beautiful spring day they are covered in clouds of white blossom.

It's beautiful out here, near the sea. Lyn and Robert love it too. That's why they took the package offered by the government when their former house was condemned – immediately and without quibble.

'I just looked at Robert and he looked at me and we said yes. We had to move on.'

This house came on to the market at the right moment. Their home in Kairaki Beach had shaken to pieces in September and for five and a half months they had lived with all their household gear, two cats and the dogs in their garage. Moving away from the area was complicated since they own not just the fish, the chickens, the cats and the dogs, but two horses that are grazed nearby. It's difficult to find a rental property that will accommodate that kind of extended family.

Life had been difficult since they were woken that spring morning and Robert walked out into sewage and liquefaction up to his knees. In the dark it was not clear whether it was the beginning of a flood: perhaps the sea was washing in; perhaps the Waimakariri was building to dangerous levels.

'He came back inside and said, "We're getting out of here NOW!" '

Lyn had been listening to her little transistor radio – the one her family have always teased her about because she has it on all the

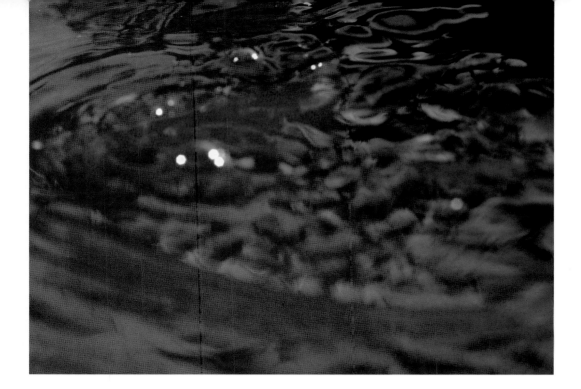

time, but this morning it proved its worth.

'I knew what was going on, that there had been a serious quake. So we left food out for the cats, got the dogs and hopped into the car and headed off inland. There were people everywhere, loading up cars, getting their kids out. And midway along the road there was this animal in the middle of the road wobbling around, all disoriented, looking around as if it was saying, "What's going on here?" I thought it was a dog, so I said to Robert, "We've got to stop and pick it up!" But it wasn't a dog, it was a sheep. I've no idea where it came from because there are no sheep around there. We couldn't fit it in so we drove on and checked up on the horses – they're in a paddock by the motorway – and they were all right so we kept driving towards Rangiora. And the strangest thing was, as soon as we passed the motorway, there was no damage! No damage at all. No cars on

the side of the road, no houses down. It just stopped, right there!'

In Rangiora they checked on the jewellery shop. There was no sign of disturbance. McDonald's was all lit up as usual. They went around to a friend's place. The power was on and their friends, a little shaken, were having a cup of tea. Lyn felt completely disoriented.

'I said to Robert, "We've got to go home, because I think I've just had the most awful dream."

When they did return to Kairaki Beach the dream was only too true. Their home was a complete mess. Volcanic eruptions of silt had left liquefied mud half a metre deep throughout their house and over the garden. Roads had cracked and slumped, leaving deep cracks and holes and snapping service pipes. Drainage ditches had collapsed, leaving the settlement vulnerable to flooding.

They also discovered their goldfish.

That was just the first of several bucket trips the goldfish have made this year.

'They were all lying there in what had been the pond in the garden with their little noses poking up through all this liquefaction. So we took buckets and got some cleanish water out of the drain and rescued them.' That was just the first of several bucket trips the goldfish have made this year, before arriving this week in their smart new quarters in the clawfoot bath on the sunny back lawn.

The house at Kairaki was clearly uninhabitable, with its silt, and its floors uphill and down and all the windows broken. There was no alternative but to hook up their camper-trailer: it was in the garage, all packed and ready, dating from the time 'when things were normal' and every weekend they could manage was spent camping.

'I kept it packed,' says Lyn. 'Food and everything, so we could just get up and go.'

When the quake destroyed their home of six years they got up and went. For a couple of weeks they parked the camper-trailer in the driveway of a friend's place in Rangiora, before deciding that the most sensible solution would be to return to their home at Kairaki. With their dogs and cats and fish they moved into the garage. It was cramped, unlined, but packed with all their things, their bed and a camping gas stove for cooking, it was to be their home for the next 12 months.

'We're demon campers. We were used to camping so we had all the gear,' says Lyn. They were better prepared than others they knew who found themselves without cooking facilities and without the wood-burning fires that had been removed over the preceding few years as part of a council initiative to provide clean air.

Lyn and Robert could cook for themselves. They even managed to produce meals for the helicopter crews and volunteers working around the city.

Moving away from the area was complicated since they own fish, chickens, cats, dogs, horses . . .

'I heard a request on the radio at work, so another girl and I went to the butcher's and got a side of mutton all cut up and some sausages. I thought, "Now, what would I feel like if I didn't have a way to cook? Something nice and warm and spicy!" '

Curried sausages, tasty casseroles: plating up 52 meals a day in a box and taking them out to the airport in Rangiora for distribution.

'It was like being back on the farm, cooking for shearers.' Lyn put a label with her name on the box. A friend in Christchurch rang to say, "You'll never guess, but my brother's just sitting down to one of your dinners!" That was a good feeling.'

Nevertheless, it was an enormously stressful time.

'We were supposed to contact the assessors and the insurers to arrange for repairs to our house and lodge claims: but you'd get

through to some call centre somewhere and they'd have no idea. They'd say, "Email us." But how were we meant to do that with no power? No computer? The phone coming into the garage only spasmodically? They kept saying, "It's quicker if you email us." I felt like ramming the phone down their throats. Honestly, if it hadn't been for my employer and my workmates, I would never have got through.'

At work she was able to use the phone to make those essential calls. Friends dropped into the shop to see if she and Robert were okay. Complete strangers enquired. When she got home at night she would sometimes find little packages left on the step: chocolate, a packet of Lifesavers, cards with drawings or inspirational sayings from her parish church, St Bartholomew's, or groups like the Salvation Army or Rotary. Her boss at the jewellery shop shouted all his staff a day trip,

flying them up to Wellington, complete with some pocket money to go shopping. She took great courage from such gestures.

'One day I had made so many phone calls and I just didn't understand what was happening. I didn't know where money was coming from or how we were going to get our lives back together. I couldn't find out the simplest things like how much it would cost to make emergency repairs like getting water put on to the house: I could see the council workers doing the repairs on the road – but I was really anxious that any repairs done on our property would cost us personally a huge amount. Robert was out of work at the time and it was a complete nightmare. Phone calls weren't being returned and if I did get through they wouldn't know what was going on. So I went to this place in Kaiapoi where they had staff to help with information and that kind of thing. I had all my papers and

I was feeling just so fragile and I said to the woman, "I need to see somebody and if you can't put up with tears, then don't talk to me!" I'd had it. And this lovely lady – June – helped me. The volunteers there were just amazing.'

Daily life took some organisation. They took showers in the rugby clubrooms at Kaiapoi and accepted food packages when they were offered, though it was hard to do so. 'But you're not functioning properly,' she says, recalling that time. 'You just can't cope. There are times when you can't even talk to people.' When life was stressful before the quake, her garden had offered solace, but now it was buried in toxic sludge. She set about rescuing as many plants as she could, putting them in pots. She went for long walks along the beach. The aftershocks were disturbing. When large ones hit and the dogs began to freak out, Lyn took them outside

and sat with them in the shade-house until they were all calm.

At this stage the general expectation was that houses at Kairaki Beach would eventually be repaired, though it was becoming clear that this was going to be a very long process.

By Christmas they needed a break. They took the trailer and went camping at the mouth of the Rangitata, a place they had visited before, but now more attractive than ever as a place for a change of pace.

'We just needed to get away. It was the best thing we did, because it was normal. It was just ordinary. At home all the lampposts were on a lean, fences were broken, there were all these constant reminders whenever you looked around. So it was good being somewhere undamaged. And on the way home I looked out the window of the car and I thought, "All those trees are still standing. Nature's still intact. It's just human buildings that have broken." It felt like reality time. It made us feel better.'

Lyn returned to work.

'I loved being there. I like the people I work with but I also just loved going in and leaving all this mess behind and being in the shop with all these beautiful things around me. The glass cabinets and rings and all the jewellery and everything. They made me feel good.'

In their garage Lyn and Robert carried on in this complicated new world of zoning, insurance and repairs to basic infrastructure. She was deeply impressed by the workers who struggled to restore essential services to the beachside settlements, fixing old sewerage pipes and mending power lines.

'There was this man: I'd see him day after day, working on the pipes across the road. He'd be there at 7.30am when I went out to work in the morning, and he'd still be there

when I got back at night. He didn't leave till 10 o'clock. And he'd have had a family to go back to, a house that was maybe broken.'

She took the work gangs hot chips to say thank you.

By February, with huge effort and at great expense the Waimakariri District Council's workers had almost restored all services to their area. Then on the 22nd everything jolted back to square one.

Lyn was at work when the jewellery cabinets began to rattle.

'We raced around, shutting up the shop, getting ready to evacuate, when this lady came banging on the door and said, "Are you shut? I want to buy a battery." And we said, "Look: there's been an earthquake." But she insisted; she came in and we had to go past all the glass cabinets to fetch her battery. She hadn't felt it because she was driving, so, as far as she was concerned it hadn't happened.'

Lyn, on the other hand, was only too well aware that it had happened. This time there was no talk of repairs to their home at Kairaki. The whole area was zoned red. All the houses in the little settlement were to be demolished and the land would revert to its natural state on the banks of the Waimakariri. Homeowners were presented with a package from the government. They could sell their property to the government at its 2007 Rating Valuation and move, or sell just the land to the government and negotiate with their individual insurance company for the value of the building.

The community at Kairaki had been close and it was hard to contemplate leaving. Some of their neighbours wanted to stay and challenge the zoning decision but Lyn was certain that there was no option. It was vitally important to be honest, to acknowledge that staying on was just not

feasible and get on with the business of relocating.

Lyn and Robert accepted the package and began the hunt for a new home. It had to be within their restricted budget, it had to be flexible, and of wooden construction – not brick or concrete. It had to have room for their animals. They wanted to stay in the area, near the beach. They wanted space for a garden. They wanted to remain close to the life they had built together in Kaiapoi.

'We'd started going in to the Working Men's Club in Kaiapoi on Friday nights. I love it. There's a fishing club, a group that are going to go to the races in Methven – we'll all get a bus and travel together. It's our community.'

A friend at work told them about this house at Pines Beach. It was small but it was solidly built and it had that big garden and the pines with the sand track down to the beach. They saw it on Monday, made an

immediate offer – thanks to bridging finance from the BNZ – and by the end of the week they owned this house, only a couple of kilometres from their old one. 'One of the men from the club, a retired building inspector, came over and had a look at the place. He knew our circumstances and he said, "Lyn, you've done well!" I was so grateful to him.'

Now they are here, and life is beginning to settle to its new pattern. Robert has a job driving for Allied Pickford in the city. Lyn continues to work at the jeweller's. Her experience with EQC and the insurers has also persuaded her to begin volunteering.

'I'm a strong person and I was having trouble coping, and I kept thinking, "What about those people who aren't so strong? How are they handling all this?" '

She began visiting for the council, handing out their flyers, telling people what was available to help them with insurance claims

'I'm a strong person and I was having trouble coping. What about those people who aren't so strong?'

and making sure they were coping.

'Sometimes they just wanted to talk. There was one old man who talked and talked until I had to say, "Look, there's a whole team of people out there waiting for me, I've got to go!" I left knowing the whole history of Kaiapoi! His house was a wreck; he was living in a single room. But it didn't matter how bad things were, everyone said, "But there's so many worse off than me." '

The year has been exhausting.

'I feel tired. There's a fundraiser for Orana Wildlife Park. Normally I'd love to help but I have to be firm this year and say no. Not right now.'

But at least they are no longer living in the garage.

She thinks a lot about how this event has unfolded and what it means for people in general. On her trip to Wellington with the staff from the jewellery shop she saw an eco-house that some students were building at the university for an international architectural competition.

'I really liked it. I think that's what Christchurch should be looking at: buildings that are easy on nature. We've just gone along thinking we can do everything our way – but nature is bigger than us and in situations like we're in now, well, you just have to stand and

let her do whatever she wants. You don't have a choice.'

The dogs are becoming restless so we take them out through the gate in the back fence onto the sand track through the pines for a run. Other people are walking dogs and we stop to chat while Buster and Bear meet their new neighbours.

Lyn is glad to be here, glad they made the move and just got on with it.

'The house is small but it's comfortable, and I've got my garden.'

She calls it her 'Survival Garden'. It is filled with the plants she has finally been

able to unpot after their long winter: plants she's 'carted about' from one garden to another. Plants she brought down from the North Island 20 years ago when she moved to Canterbury; plants that once belonged in Robert's mother's garden. They seem to be doing well in their new location.

But best of all, says Lyn, is that 'when I get up in the morning and put the jug on, there are lambs across the road in that paddock. When you see lambs running about you think, well, things can't be too bad. You can't be sad when there are lambs around!'

'A sense of hope . . . Just sitting in the sun listening to beautiful classical music amidst all the devastation.'

Sally Blundell

Before we talk, Sally shows me the foundations of her home on Fifield Terrace. It's a solid, kindly house constructed during World War I that they have altered and modified over the past 15 years. It stands on the terrace above the Heathcote River where it winds slowly through Opawa between willows and elms. A line of white paint on the concrete marks the original baseline of the weatherboard walls. Now the line is separated from the walls by a good 5cm where the ground beneath has slumped toward the river, taking the foundations with it. In the kitchen she peels back sticky tape to expose the tear that opened across the width of the house.

'It's like a wound,' she says, and that is exactly right. The tape pulls away like elastoplast.

Along the hallway, paintings stand with their faces turned to the wall. This is a house of paintings. Sally writes regular reviews of exhibitions as part of her work as a freelance journalist. She has spent a lifetime looking closely at the work of New Zealand's artists. Her husband David is a picture framer and shares her passion. By the desk where she works, looking out to the river, hang canvases by Philip Trusttum, Joanna Braithwaite, Mark Braunias, Peter Robinson, Kathryn Madill.

Elsewhere there are gaps on the wall.

'We've taken down the Zina Swanson works twice – once after September, and again after the February quake. But I think it might be time to put them back.'

We settle to talk in this room surrounded by paintings on a cool September morning, Bridie the shaggy collie-cross asleep at our feet.

Sally is measured and thoughtful. 'I've been thinking about September,' she says,

> *'We made cups of tea, lit candles and for two hours until it was light we sat around talking. It was weirdly nice.'*

'and all I could think of was that it was like when you were a child putting on plays and when the really scary thing happened, you turned the lights on and off very quickly. David was saying "Get up! Get up!" And before I'd quite woken up I was lurching out of bed and down the hallway.' Their two sons were home at the time. They all gathered in the kitchen.

'There was no power and everything smelled of vinegar because a bottle had smashed on the floor. We couldn't find batteries for the torch – we were totally unprepared – but the gas was working so we made cups of tea, lit candles and for two hours until it was light we sat around talking. It was actually weirdly nice. We were together as a family and that doesn't happen very often now that the boys are in their twenties. We just sat in the kitchen, talking.'

What did they talk about, sitting at the kitchen table in the dark?

'It probably sounds strange, but we talked about myths and legends – stories we used to tell the children when they were small. Icelandic stories, volcanic explosions, apocalyptic tales.' Ragnarok. The final battle between gods and frost giants and the wolf Skoll who swallowed the sun before the earth sank into the sea and the old era ended.

When dawn came they were finally able to examine the damage to their home: the entire contents of the pantry on the floor, furniture fallen, books and objects scattered and broken. 'It was so good to see the sky lighten and the sun come up. We were cold and that was when it finally felt safe enough to go back to bed.'

Without power or transistor radio they had no idea of the wider damage, but in an hour or so the phone calls began. Family calls from Waikanae, Hastings, Australia, the

UK – where the television news had begun broadcasting images of the quake.

'They knew so much more than us. We could hardly tell them anything.'

Later in the morning they went out for a walk, talking to other people emerging from their homes, checking up on neighbours.

'There was a lot of 'You okay?' 'Yes, we're okay. Are you okay?' It was like coming up into this strange new world. You didn't know what to expect. We stayed close to home all day and had dinner with neighbours that night. There was the clustering around the kitchen table, then this neighbourhood clustering. Everyone was stunned by the size of what had happened and of course there were still aftershocks happening – but over the next few days we began to hear more and it seemed that no one had been killed. It was as if we'd got through it. We'd survived.'

Only once did Sally experience panic: out walking along the riverbank one morning she was shaken by a large aftershock and was suddenly overwhelmed by a sense that absolutely anything could happen.

'There were all these stories – that the peninsula volcanoes were reactivating, for instance – and for just a couple of minutes I felt total fear.' The kind of fear she detected in drawings by primary-age children in an exhibition staged a short time after the quake by Christchurch's gallery of contemporary art, COCA. Over and over again the children drew the same image: a monster, a big dog under a bed. Something down there was alive and menacing. It made complete sense from a child's perspective and for just a couple of minutes on the riverbank it made complete sense too to the adult Sally, despite the fact that she was by then writing articles about the quake for various publications, interviewing scientists and structural engineers. And

She was suddenly
overwhelmed
by a sense that
absolutely
anything could
happen.

despite years of personal experience of smaller quakes and jolts. She grew up in Lower Hutt and later lived in Wellington. 'So I thought I knew all about quakes. But I wasn't prepared for the aftershocks and that overwhelming fear, well … I rationalised it, I pulled myself back, but it was just a horrible place to be.'

Daily life resumed. Sally continued to write, seated at her desk working as the shocks rippled through. 'It seemed like a strange thing to be doing, reviewing an exhibition or working on a story while this massive tectonic thing was happening under my feet. But writing about the quake, learning about the science of it, reading avidly every article in the *Press* actually helped. There was an order to earthquakes, a sequence, a framework that was reassuring. And my desk is good and sturdy. I felt safe there. But I'd be interviewing someone in Auckland and – whoops! there's another

one! – and we'd just carry on. Two completely different worlds.'

She was at her desk at 12.51 on February 22 when the ceiling light – a heavy shade not prone to movement – began swinging violently and the entire contents of an old sideboard crashed to the floor. The violent jolting that afternoon was a re-run of the previous experience – but this time the house shifted on its foundations, and the aftermath felt different. In September, the staff at the local supermarket were handing out chocolates to children the next day. This time the supermarket collapsed completely. Liquefaction poured onto the roads, and that crack opened in Sally's kitchen. No water. No power. No sewerage. The next day a dry nor'west gale was blowing and a truck came to their neighbourhood, dispensing water. Sally and her sister-in-law gathered up buckets and bottles.

'We went around the corner and it was such a bizarre sight: there was this blue blue sky, this dusty road and all these people hurrying with Coke bottles and Pump bottles – anything they could grab – for water. It seemed so archaic. There was water everywhere – springs had broken out on all sides, pipes had burst and the river was running high – but here we were, frantic for water. It was so desperate.'

Sally wanted nothing but to get out of the city. She needed to escape. So the next day, after cleaning up David's workplace, they drove to Fairlie. Just for a couple of days, but she was able to have a shower, to wash her hair and also, for the first time, to see TV footage of the devastation elsewhere in the city. She encountered small but memorable acts of kindness: a restaurant voucher from the owners of the Aorangi Motel, an offer of a free room at Lake Tekapo, a hug from a

fellow refugee they met at a service station.

Such things left them feeling calmer and stronger, so with the boot of the car filled with batteries, groceries and emergency supplies they headed back to the city and a life that had become determinedly physical. Every two or three days they crossed town to have a shower at a friend's place, and do the washing. Sally recalls the people she saw when she was out walking the dog, repairing what had already been broken in September, shovelling silt, putting the letterbox straight again.

'Here were all these human beings who had been knocked over and they were simply getting back up again. It wasn't exactly inspiring. It didn't show Christchurch courage or some special provincial spirit, nothing like that. It was just overwhelming in its automatic nature. We just seemed like very little people, getting on with the job at hand while the Port Hills juddered and jolted.'

Sally was working on a story about New Zealand herbs but she found it terribly hard to concentrate – and large amounts of material had been deleted from her computer. Deadlines passed, and meanwhile the quaking was constant and distracting. A family on Opawa Road had an artesian bore on their property that they made available to anyone who needed water.

'It became routine, this trip to collect the day's supplies. You'd stand in the queue, chat, exchange experience or tips, walk home with the bucket filled. It was great. Those people deserve a huge thank you.'

When the aftershock hit in June little changed visibly, but Sally felt a seismic shift in the mood of people around her.

'It became darker. When I went to Opawa for water no one talked much. It felt like, "Here we go again. Nothing is going to come right. It's not just going to be a

straightforward progress to recovery. Not a straight upward line at all." '

And now, a year later? How does it seem?

There is sadness, and loss.

'At that exhibition at COCA where I saw the children's drawings of the monster under the bed, someone had exhibited a simple carton of eggs – one dozen – except they had removed one of the eggs. That is how the city feels to me at present: as if all these fragile structures are being broken, and they are being broken too fast, too soon. They are demolishing buildings when they should just fence them off, let them stand a little longer, so we can come to terms with them and decide what to do. Every time I go over the bridge into town I see the Basilica. I'm not Catholic but I remember how excited my children were when they recognised it in Gavin Bishop's *Mrs Maginty and the Bizarre Plant*, and it's sad to see it being lifted down bit by bit by cranes.'

There is indecision. Their house, where they have lived for 16 years, may be deemed unrepairable by the insurers and demolished. The ground itself may be ruled unsafe.

A year after they were jolted from bed to sit around the kitchen table, telling old stories of apocalypse, the family lives with daily uncertainty.

But then there are other moments.

'Soon after the September earthquake I was walking along Colombo Street. Quite a few shops had been demolished, including this little Mexican place we used to go to. And there were some people on the site: there were deckchairs and a little caravan selling coffee and a couple of people were playing cellos. I found out later it was a Gapfiller event, but at the time I didn't realise. It was just the most wonderful feeling. A sense of hope, like a weed growing out of a crack. Just sitting in the sun listening to beautiful

classical music amidst all the devastation.'

There has been the inspiration of the public talks she has attended on architecture and what might be done to rebuild a beautiful and architecturally arresting Christchurch. And there was a moment on St Asaph Street.

'They had demolished some big buildings and I looked up and there was the back view of all the shops on High Street – a view I'd never seen before. In a strange way they looked charming, like something out of *Coronation Street*. It often feels to me in a

way as if we're getting a glimpse of the real Christchurch, the one that always lay behind the one we knew. I mean, when I first came here in 1983 it felt like something out of the fifties: the "Garden City" with its floral clocks. But now we're seeing the reality of it, which is a wetland with streams and springs. It's still a garden – but it's a very different garden from the one we thought we were living in.'

Bev Prout and Quentin Wilson

When I arrive on Saturday morning at the house Bev Prout and Quentin Wilson are renting in St Albans, Bev is waiting on the step.

'You've timed it right,' she says. Their house – vacated eight months ago after the February quake – was arsoned in the early hours of Friday morning. 'I got a message on my answerphone from one of our neighbours at 2am.'

The neighbour is famously direct.

'Bev: Philip here. Your house is burning. Cheers, Phil.'

Despite everything, Bev laughs at the familiar directness and that concluding 'Cheers!' as we drive through Edgeware. At first sight it could be Saturday morning in any New Zealand suburb. The butcher's is open, cyclists head out for a ride towards Brighton, people wander back from the dairy with the *Weekend Press*. There are gaps: a

tarpaulin over a roof, a cleared section that might recently have been a house, shops with their windows still taped over. We turn south toward the river. The trees are bigger here, and covered in spring leaf. The street winds, following the contours of a creek. On its banks are big Victorian and Edwardian villas, some dating from the era of orchards and riverside farms, interspersed with postwar state houses. A little knot of people is gathered on the footpath opposite an urban park with slides and a swimming pool set among the trees.

There is Quentin, wearing a hard hat and orange vest, talking with an elderly couple. There's a small boy on a scooter, mesmerised by all the activity. There's a woman with a large dog. A work van is pulled up at the kerb, with a tangle of cabling and gear in the rear. A crane lifts its dinosaur head among the trees, there's the racket of chainsaws and

75

heavy machinery, and there are workmen moving about the burnt-out shell of what was until a few months ago a home. A large two-storey house, bought 17 years ago, with ample room to accommodate a blended family: Bev and Quentin, Bev's four teenage children, and Quentin's elderly mother. The couple shared a love of old houses.

'My head says minimalist, modern, easy care,' says Bev, 'but my heart always says big, old, high-stud, draughty Victorian. Ever since I was a child I've loved Victorian houses. My mother just said, "All that dusting!" But that was the house Quentin and I both wanted.'

A house with a past. A house lived in 70 years ago by the elderly man who is talking to Quentin out on the footpath. It turns out that he grew up here, living in this house for over 20 years. He had learned of the arson from a son who works with the fire brigade, and decided to drive over with his wife to say

goodbye. He tells Quentin about the Dutch lads who boarded with the family back in the 1950s, how people round about were asked to billet these young emigrant lads and teach them English. The lads in return had taught him how to swear in Dutch.

The crane grips and strains at blackened timbers and crumpled roofing iron. The noise is deafening. Something is waving high up among the burnt timbers on the second floor.

'One of my scarves,' says Bev. She had seen them yesterday when she looked up from the burnt-out porch and could see all the way through the shell of the house to their former bedroom. Her scarves were still folded on the shelves, their clothes still hung in the wardrobe. The scarf waves from a charred floor joist like a little banner.

A couple of workmen emerge from the ruins carrying a piece of furniture.

'My sideboard!' says Bev.

She likes that sideboard. She had spent hours buffing its timber to a glossy sheen. It was the perfect size to contain her collection of jack-in-the-boxes. Now it stands in the garden beneath a rhododendron, dusty but intact. Inside there is some china – just some random plates, a jug, some circles of glass Bev and Quentin take a minute to recognise: they're the rims of martini glasses.

'No problem there,' says Quentin. 'Watch us spot a martini glass from a hundred paces!'

The fire was probably started outside his former study on the ground floor, where once he had worked as a book designer and publishing consultant. The woman with the dog says darkly that it was probably a kid who lived nearby; she knows the kid, there have been other fires lately … The crane heaves an entire windowframe into the air. It is massive, with those ornate Edwardian volutes and three huge panes. Once it framed the view of the river from their bedroom upstairs.

'I loved those windows,' Bev says. 'We fixed them so they opened properly, top and bottom, and in spring, about now, we'd open the top one and have this lovely fresh air all summer. When you were lying in bed at night you could hear the sound of the leaves.'

She takes me on a short walk along the riverbank past the houses of their neighbours: most are deserted, all are destined for demolition, if the arsonist kid doesn't get them first. They slump at ungainly angles amid magnolias in full flower. Huge cracks have opened across their yards. We return just as the kitchen wall falls away in one charred and melted piece. Bev and Quentin have had enough. They'll come back later, but right now, they don't want to be here. We go back to their rented house with its strangely uncluttered rooms and sit at the rented table to talk.

First: September.

'I thought we were going to die,' says Bev, 'upstairs in that house. I couldn't believe it would withstand the shaking. I didn't think of it as an earthquake: just this huge apocalyptic event. When the shaking stopped we had a look around. My youngest son Nick had just bought a torch app for his phone – he was really pleased to be able to use that.'

They also had a little emergency kit downstairs in the kitchen with torches and batteries and a radio. Some years ago Quentin had published a book on surviving bird flu and had taken its 'be prepared' message to heart.

'It was good,' says Bev, 'because right from the start we had a line to the outside world. National Radio, Sean Plunket – they were absolutely fantastic and I also found out what was going on via texts from a friend whose sister was in Sydney and could see the television footage. We didn't see that ourselves till the power came on late the next afternoon.'

Although severely shaken, the house had remained intact and largely undamaged. But it rattled sufficiently in the repeated after-shocks to make it seem wise to set up interim camp on the porch. Meanwhile, only a few blocks away, Bev's daughter Stephanie, who was pregnant at the time, had barely regis-tered the quake at all. She and her husband had remained snugly in bed and in the morning found the only disturbance in their entire house was that a roll of paper towelling had fallen from a bench and unspooled across the kitchen floor.

'It was the same later on at work,' says Bev. 'It was as if we inhabited a parallel universe. Some people had experienced virtually noth-ing, and they didn't get why I was in shock, stumbling over words and forgetting things.'

Over the next few days, people turned up with water. Despite being only metres from the Avon River, they had no safe drinking supply. Sewerage pipes had burst and poured muck into the system. Friends from the country, friends of their children, even complete strangers arrived with containers full – unasked but somehow knowing instinctively that that was the most wonderfully useful thing they could do. There were other little kindnesses: their neighbour Philip turned up the next morning with coffee on a tray – proper coffee. People left little packages on the front doorstep: a bar of chocolate, a bottle of water.

Adjustments were made. Bev and Quentin never again slept in their upstairs bedroom with its windows open to the spring leaves. They didn't quite trust the cracks across the ornate plaster ceiling. They moved instead to the lounge downstairs, sleeping on sofas in sleeping bags they left unzipped so that they could make a run for the doorway in the larger shocks. The dog and two cats slept beside them.

'They learned the drill quickly,' says Bev. 'At the slightest rattle they were up and off. We must have looked so funny, all of us fighting to get into the doorway at once. The animals thought it was a great game.'

But in general the whole period between the two major quakes is vague – the effect of a general mental disengagement they recognise as an effect of the quake. Both returned to work, Bev as manager of the City Library in the central city, Quentin to his study and the business of books and their design.

Christmas came around – traditionally a major family occasion, everyone gathered on the deck of the old house, a day recorded and photographed each year. But neither Bev nor Quentin can remember Christmas 2010. It's

a blur. Earthquake brain. The Boxing Day shock caused a little upset, but it was not until February 22 that everything changed utterly.

Quentin was at home, working in his study. He ran out into the hallway as the room exploded and heavy bookcases that had been firmly secured to every wall simply snapped from their restraints, depositing half a metre of books over floor and desk and chair. Dust obscured everything. A neighbour came over but Quentin has no memory of what they talked about. With his cellphone battery flat, he does recall trying to repair the analogue phones and attempting to find Bev, who had been at lunch on Worcester Boulevard in the central city. She had emerged from beneath a table and set off immediately for the library to check on her colleagues. She recalls passing on the way a rank of scooters parked outside Caffé Roma: all pastel colours, pink and blue and green, and all flipped neatly sideways like a pack of cards, in an odd new kind of order. The image remains weirdly vivid in her memory of the day.

'Everyone had evacuated the library, but lots wanted to go back in to get their handbags and keys and it was really awful. People were saying, "But I live in Kaiapoi!" "I live on Huntsbury Hill!" They just had to set off on foot. And then all these people started streaming past with awful faces – white, with staring eyes –it was like footage of people escaping genocide. And I kept worrying

*The room exploded and heavy
bookcases snapped from their restraints,
depositing half a metre of books over
floor and desk and chair.*

about one of the large windows onto the street that had broken: I didn't know then that the whole CBD was going to be closed down. Anyway, eventually all the library people had gone and I decided to walk home. There were three of us, in among all these other people, walking. The traffic was gridlocked, cars were parked, abandoned

anywhere. Everyone was just stunned.'

She reached home around six. At first, approaching the house from the back via a shortcut knee-deep in liquefaction, she thought perhaps all might be well.

'Then I came around to the front and there was Quentin. He'd opened all the doors and I could see there was plaster down everywhere – a complete mess. Philip came over with wine and we stood outside and I asked him, in his professional capacity – he's an architect – what he thought. And he said, 'It's fucked.'

Bev and Quentin laugh about it now, seated in their rented kitchen, remembering. That darkly tinted, tough, realistic, post-quake laughter.

They moved out into a tent on the back lawn for several days. Then they began to move about the city: five or six times over the next six weeks they moved between the

spare rooms and sofas of friends and family. Eventually they found this rental house in St Albans. For 12 months the rent is covered by insurance. After that, who knows? They have been patient thus far. As a manager herself, Bev has been well aware of how very complex this whole organisational process must be. But her blood pressure is high for the first time in her life and in the weeks before the announcement of the fate of their house she became anxious.

So much depended upon it.

Their house was red-zoned – or 'redded' to use local parlance. Demolition was inevitable. The fire simply accelerated the process – but it allowed no time for adjustment, no time to retrieve those coats and scarves and tumbled books and furniture, no time for Bev's daughter to return from London and see for herself what had happened to her old home.

It will be two years before the City

Library is reopened and months before they have a permanent home.

'I used to be a real estate junkie,' Bev says. 'I liked looking at properties on the internet, thinking "Ooh, we could live there!" Or "That place looks great!" but now that I actually have to think about finding a new house I can't get excited about it.'

They're weary.

So what keeps them going a year after the room heaved them from their bed?

Grandchildren: Bev's granddaughter, Clara, born 10 days after the first quake. Quentin's grandchildren, to whom he talks regularly on Skype. And work: Quentin likes the steady flow of book design, working with his daughter Antoinette, who is a book editor in the Wairarapa. Bev works to make the city's libraries function. She takes pleasure in the fact that the South City Library is operating once more, and that there have not so far been any staff losses. Librarians as employees of the city council have been redeployed. They direct trucks at the refill sites around the city for example, or help out operating IT for the recovery of sewerage and power systems.

Friends have made life tolerable too. And laughter. That dark and hilarious post-quake laughter.

Two days after we meet to talk, Bev emails me. She had gone into a shop to find out the value of some candlesticks for their insurance claim: it's so difficult, she says, trying to remember absolutely everything that was in their house, in cupboards and on shelves.

'The owner looked at me and said, "How's your house?" And then he saw my face and he said, "It's toast, I suppose?" '

The colloquialism couldn't have been more apt. And, despite all the grief at losing her home and the deep sadness brought by this extraordinary year, Bev laughed.

It was the perfect size to contain her collection of jack-in-the-boxes.

Heidi, Rick and Erik Cassells Brown,

'For boys like him this year has been great: diggers everywhere, holes in the road, things that need fixing.'

Erik is three. He is wearing blue overalls with the orange high-vis of the demolition crews. He has on an orange plastic hard hat. His grandmother made those overalls for him. He wears them everywhere: riding his two-wheeler full tilt up and down the footpath (he has just learned how to stand up and pedal); playing the ukulele he calls a guitar, strumming properly, with a pick. And he wears the overalls when knocking at a concrete block wall in the garden with a rubber mallet. He has an imaginary friend called Tin who will give him a hand – he helps with all Erik's projects. Erik stands back, sizing up the job. He says, 'Think we'll take that down tomorrow.' He tells his mother he is 'doing earthquake repairs'. That means taking his hammer and knocking holes in the living-room wall.

Down the road, towards the hills, there are slumps in the road and houses with tarpaulin still over holes in the roof. But for Erik this is all fascinating stuff.

'For boys like him,' says Heidi, 'this year has been great: diggers everywhere, holes in the road, things that need fixing.'

Not that it is exactly adventure. Erik is very serious about the destruction and well aware of what is happening around him. He has gone with his mother and father to see the CBD and knows what the piles of rubble mean. 'Oh no!' he says. 'That's fallen down!' He and Tin have a lot of work ahead of them.

His home in Beckenham has escaped largely unscathed. A bookshelf fell against the front door and smashed the glass, but otherwise there are only minor cracks. It is a new home for the family, purchased in January. Before that they rented a place at Brighton while planning to build an eco-home on a hilly piece of land at Little River. Rick is studying civil engineering at Canterbury, and

operates a business contracting to the council to do pest control and track maintenance about the city and peninsula. (Erik breaks in here, eager to remind us of a bridge at Cass Bay that is broken – the steps are all broken.) Heidi is a landscape architect.

Both reacted quickly on the morning of September 4 when the quake rattled their rented place at Brighton. They grabbed Erik and found safety under a table, well drilled throughout childhood in the routine.

'A friend of mine from Germany had no idea what was happening and just froze. But we both knew to get under something strong.' The house, a 'rickety old bach', shook mightily and as soon as they could move they raced next door to their landlord's, whose home was more solidly constructed. (As we talk, Erik is building a tower of wooden blocks on the living-room carpet. His toy digger and a crane are lined up under the desk, waiting.)

'The thing we were worried about was tsunami. All we could hear were cars starting up all around us in the dark and racing: not just driving, but gunning it, getting out,' says Rick. A neighbour told him later about driving over the Causeway towards the hills and how he was definitely airborne for part of it, over huge holes and a bridge that had risen half a metre. They themselves stayed put, having learned from a friend's text message that the epicentre was not out at sea but inland and therefore unlikely to cause tsunami. It was a matter of weighing up one unknown – the state of the roads between Brighton and the hills – against another.

They stayed home, dosed themselves up on homoeopathic remedies, drank tea, wrapped themselves warmly in sleeping bags. And early in the afternoon they went for a bike ride around Brighton. By the jetty they met Swedish friends who told them of going

'*I just wanted to stay quiet. I mean,
I'd thought the world was going
to end.*'

down to the beach at dawn that morning and finding that the sand, normally sloping, had settled to being completely flat and all the little pipis and cockles lay exposed.

'They said there were clouds of seabirds, masses of them, a complete feeding frenzy – and it was so beautiful,' says Heidi. 'They were going out whenever there was a shock and seeing what was happening. I thought that was amazing but I couldn't do it myself. I just wanted to stay quiet. I mean, I'd thought the world was going to end. I'd knelt under the table thinking, "I hope somebody nice finds Erik and that they'll look after him well."'

(Erik is driving his digger into the tower. It falls with a satisfying clatter, to general applause. He starts building it all over again.)

What did they do then? Rick drove out late that afternoon to Little River to fetch a generator, a freaky drive down broken roads.

But after a few days with power but no water or sewage they decided to leave the city. They headed south to stay with family in Wanaka and Milton.

'There was just no point in struggling on. That first night away we both woke up thinking the whole room was shaking and I thought, "My god, we're having a quake here and if it's this bad here, what's it like at home?" That happened for several nights.' On the way back to Christchurch three weeks later, they met a family from Christchurch at Omarama who said they had experienced exactly the same phenomenon of phantom night quakes.

They moved from the rented bach to a tent on the land at Little River, but in January found this house in Beckenham which they were able to rent until they could arrange its purchase.

Five weeks after they had moved in,

Heidi and Erik were in the kitchen when the ground jolted. She had planned to go into the city but a friend had dropped in unexpectedly so they were fortunately not in a downtown carpark as planned but once more able to take refuge under the dining table.

It is a beautiful table, made by Rick from pale speckled oak. He would, in an ideal world, be not an engineer but a maker of wooden furniture. It is plain, rectangular and four-legged with a drawer in the narrow end that slides smoothly on its runners. It is beautiful, perfectly crafted – but in this context, more importantly, it was also very, very solid. Heidi knelt on hands and knees beneath its secure frame, over Erik who lay beneath her. She noticed that there was a brief pause between aftershocks: a little 30-second gap when she was able to run out and rescue things. Like the bookshelves Rick was building which had toppled and

threatened to break other things. Somehow she was strong enough at that instant to lift them away and rest them safely on their sides. She rescued the computer, while Erik stayed safe under his dad's table. They sang. Lullabies mostly. 'Twinkle Twinkle Little Star' with all the verses: Erik gets cross when they sing only the first verse and miss out the bits about the traveller in the dark being grateful for the star's tiny spark. They sang an African lullaby, one they have sung to Erik since he was a baby: Husha my baby. Husha husha my baby. They remained there 'for ages' until Heidi heard a friend calling, 'Are you all right?'

'I called, "Why aren't you under your table?" and she said, "We can't fit under our table – it's round with a big central stem."' And they had their granny from Samoa. They were sitting out on the street instead, where they all felt safe. So we got all the

chocolate out of the cupboard and we went and joined them at their place.'

The greatest worry at that point was the failure of the cellphone system.

'I had no idea where Rick was and my friend didn't know what had happened to her husband who works near the airport. I thought cellphones were supposed to function in emergencies, but they're a hopeless technology.'

Her friend's husband was on his way home on foot, a journey that took several hours. And Rick, too, was safe.

'I was in the Rutherford Building at the university. It was one of the first buildings in Christchurch to be engineered back in the 1960s to withstand an earthquake. It's a massive long structure in three pieces and all three swayed and knocked into one another. I was in the stairwell and only on the second floor so I could run. You could hear all the glass smashing in the chemistry labs and people screaming.'

In a 4WD, bouncing over traffic islands, he headed for home across the city. It took three and a half hours.

'I wished I'd taken my bike that day. It would have taken a quarter of the time under those conditions.'

(Erik is making a workshop behind the easy chair, arranging all his tools. He takes a break to ask me what kind of car I drive. I say a Subaru and he is pleased. That's his favourite kind.)

That night they shared a meal with their neighbours. Others turned up – friends and relatives. They sang. Many of the children attended the same playgroup and knew the same songs. The singing, says Heidi, had the effect of calming everyone. The children played together, and afterwards Heidi, Rick and Erik slept together outside in a tent on

*'I just focus on each day.
I've just got the energy
for each day.'*

the lawn. The next day Heidi went with their neighbour to find drinking water. They drove about the city, until they found a tanker delivering water at a school in Philipstown.

'There were queues of people, right around the block. And I thought, "This is hopeless."'

She knew what was coming: the aftershocks, the broken roads, the absence of sewerage, the daily effort to get basic necessities like water. They had been through that already in September. Once again, the solution was to head south for the solace of family. Three and a half weeks later, after sewerage and water had been restored in their area of the city, they returned.

And now, a year after their lives changed on that September morning, how is it?

'You think you've got over the quake. You've got used to the aftershocks. Everything is back to normal,' says Heidi. 'And then

something will happen: like the other night. We were watching that Scribe video.'

(Rap artist Scribe produced a reworking of his 'Not Many', which he performed against a backdrop of the post-quake city.)

'When we heard him sing, Rick became all teary and I had my armour on but inside I felt flat. I still do, though I also feel hopeful for the beautiful forms of art that might come out of the quakes. I miss my old life. And I know because of my training that it could take a very long time before all this settles down.'

Leaving is not an option. Rick is studying, and has three more busy years before he has finished his degree. But it is something else that holds them here.

'I'm not a Cantabrian,' says Heidi, 'and neither is Rick. I'm from Otago: South Otago to be specific. Milton. And Rick is from Auckland, but I don't think we could leave

here. When we were staying in Dunedin we met this other family from here and it was so nice to be able to talk to them. I mean, people elsewhere are kind – but it felt different talking to people who'd actually gone through it, who knew exactly what we were talking about. So I just focus on each day. I've just got the energy for each day.'

She is not working professionally at present in landscape architecture but she thinks about the future shape of life here.

'I think about the city and I wonder, "How is it all going to work? What will it be like during Erik's lifetime?" '

She thinks about more than the simple reconstruction of buildings.

'I think about the air quality, because it's full of dust. And the water. The heavy

chlorination and what that might be doing to our immune systems, especially children's immune systems. We've had so many colds and bugs this past winter. Everybody has.'

She and Rick think a lot about how the city might change to be better suited to the needs of children and families, with local living and cycleways and footpaths in the place of the 60s-style car-focused city Christchurch had become.

Erik is taking a break, lying on the sofa watching *Little Bear* on DVD. His hard hat has been laid aside for now, and his rubber mallet. Beyond the living room the city waits: he's only three, but rebuilding cities takes many years.

He and Tin have plenty of time in which to make their contribution.

'It was really social. No one had any power so everybody was outside, talking.'

Helen Webby

Helen has not yet unpacked. The living room in her house in St Martins feels almost bare, without its usual crowd of harps: a little bevy of Celtic harps for teaching, a lightweight harp in brilliant blue carbonfibre for easy transport in her stationwagon and, most impressive of all, the majestic concert pedal-harp with its pillar carved in the form of a nikau palm. It's the work of her brother Kim, a renowned harp-maker in Whangarei, who created it for her in 1996. That harp is still in its custom-built travelling box after its most recent journey – to Japan. The Canterbury Symphony Orchestra, for which Helen is principal harpist, was invited by the Asia Pacific Orchestra Festival to perform at its annual festival in Tokyo, following a long succession of international orchestras to be so honoured: the Sydney Symphony, the China National Symphony Orchestra, the state orchestras of South Korea, Singapore, Vietnam, orchestras from Mongolia, Thailand …

'It was fantastic,' she says, as the cats wind around her legs, ecstatic that she's home at last. The orchestra had performed a mixed programme of standard orchestral fare – the Rachmaninov Piano Concerto No. 3 with New Zealand pianist John Chen; Finnish composer Rautavaara's 7th Symphony (*Angel of Light* – 'all epic sweeping strings, horns and brass'); and an exquisite New Zealand work, *Icescape*, by Chris Cree Brown. She scrambles in her bag with its airline tags flapping and finds the programme with its glossy photographs and text in English and Japanese. The cats demand to be petted. Friends arrive: the woman who had fed the cats while Helen was away brings back a key. Helen makes tea, feeds her cats. We talk about the tour. And music.

It has been central to this year, as it has always been central to her life. Born and raised in Whangarei, Helen has played the harp since she was 12. Her family was not especially musical, but one day at a church fair her parents bought a selection of second-hand records.

'They were those compilation disks: *100 Greatest Classical Hits*, that kind of thing.' On a recording of 'ballet hits' Helen heard a piece of music that caught her attention.

'It was a piece called "The Waltz of the Flowers". I didn't know what the instrument was that played the long introduction, but it sounded just beautiful.'

Helen had discovered the harp. She began taking lessons and when she showed marked aptitude for the instrument, her mother went to the library and found a book of plans for constructing a harp which she handed to Kim, then a 16-year-old taking woodwork at school. Helen soon had her first harp.

On leaving school she embarked on a BMus at Auckland University, specialising in harp performance, then travelled to Holland and Germany for further study, particularly under the tutelage of Maria Graf, Professor of Music at Hamburg. Helen remained in Europe for 10 years, studying, playing with chamber groups and small orchestras. She also travelled in Ireland, learning the repertoire of the Celtic harp. In 2000, via the international musicians' grapevine, she heard that the Canterbury Symphony Orchestra was planning to advertise a permanent position for a harpist. She applied and returned to New Zealand.

In the winter of 2010 she was as usual 'doing my harp thing': playing for the CSO and when required for the New Zealand Symphony Orchestra, 'zipping off and doing this and that', teaching numerous

harp students around the city. On the last Sunday in August she and flautist Tony Ferner performed the Mozart Flute and Harp Concerto with the CSO in the cathedral. A beautiful concert, coinciding with Tony's 60th birthday.

A week later the city woke to savage jolting. The initial shock roused Helen from bed to hide under the desk in her living room. When her house on the riverbank on Palatine Terrace stopped shaking she returned to bed and stayed there through the succeeding aftershocks until around 8am, when her friend Victoria turned up.

'She works in Antarctica and she happened to be passing through Christchurch on her way back down to the ice from Kerikeri, where she had stayed over the winter. She arrived outside my house with the big Antarctic van – she had the keys for the weekend. There was room for about 10 people in there

and she'd driven over – v-e-r-y slowly – all ready to evacuate me if I needed evacuating. She'd been staying in a hotel by Hagley Park where it had been quite dramatic but there was no damage. We sat in my lounge eating muesli and milk. She brought peanut butter with her for some reason, and I wanted toast and peanut butter but the power was off.'

A friend phoned.

'My friend Margaret over in Woolston called and said, "I've got power!" So we decided we'd walk over there. It was a nice sunny day.'

On the way they passed the St Martins supermarket, which was a little dishevelled but still open, so they went in and bought pink buns – 'something sociable to eat while we sat on Margaret's sofa'.

'It was interesting what people in the checkout line were buying: it was all comfort food. The man in front of me had eggs,

'There has been so much I've enjoyed this year. Maybe it's got something to do with being a musician: we never have an orderly, settled life.'

bacon, cigarettes, beer. And here we were buying pink buns. No one was buying sensible emergency rations like baked beans.'

At Margaret's house they were watching the TV coverage of destruction on a big flat-screen TV. The experience was quite surreal.

'There we were, sitting on this comfortable sofa, drinking coffee and eating pink buns and the mayor was talking about "infrastructure collapse". That was the phrase they kept repeating all day. It felt bizarre.'

In the afternoon they walked about Woolston and St Martins.

'It was really social. No one had any power so everybody was outside, talking. We passed one woman who was weeding her garden and Victoria turned to me and said, "Wow! Infrastructure collapse!"'

That night five friends gathered at Margaret and Arthur's place for a shared meal, including a woman who had been working on the fourth floor of the police building downtown and been very frightened as the structure shook about. But the mood that night was cheerful. Damage had been minimal on that side of the city. No one had been killed by the quake.

During the following weeks the Town Hall reopened for business and the orchestra could recommence its scheduled concerts. Helen continued teaching and, in particular, she continued rehearsals with her new venture: the Christchurch Harp Orchestra, a group of 20 players who were preparing for a Christmas charity concert at St Stephen's Church on Ilam Road. In February's quake the church became unusable, but in September it sustained only mild cracking and was still in use at Christmas. The concert went without a hitch.

'It was really enjoyable. And really, basically that's been the theme for this whole

year,' says Helen. 'I don't want to sound too chirrupy, but there has been so much I've enjoyed this year. Maybe it's got something to do with being a musician: we're so accustomed to dealing with irregularity and change. We never have an orderly, settled life.'

Some of her students left the city, frightened by the quake: a German family returned to Germany: a Welsh family, after suffering terrible damage out at Sumner, gave up the struggle and went back to Britain. 'Canadian Susan', who had emailed Helen some months earlier from beyond the Arctic Circle enquiring about harp lessons, returned to more stable ground in North America. But most students continued with their lessons. The music seemed to help.

'One woman said to me, "The highlight of my week now is going to the supermarket, so I need my harp lesson!" Playing the harp is very absorbing, physically and mentally. I

mean, it produces a beautiful sound, but it also requires concentration and multi-tasking. You have to think about fingering, you have to think about the notes on the page – you can't think about other things when you are playing.'

Helen was in the midst of a lesson at midday on February 22 when a massive jolt shook her house and tumbled her on top of her student.

'We both fell against one another and I could feel the bookcase behind me sliding across the wall towards the concert harp, so I was struggling to hold it back and hold the harp upright, and we were all tangled and sort of spread-eagled.' She demonstrates, legs and arms flung in opposing directions. She managed to hold the harp clear so that it sustained nothing more than a mild dent.

The city, however, was in chaos, and the CSO cancelled all concerts. With no

requirement to attend rehearsals, Helen went to Dunedin to stay with her boyfriend, folk musician Sean Manning, for a couple of weeks. The time away from her busy schedule gave her some breathing space during which she was able to commission a new work: nine composers – Lyell Cresswell, Gillian Whitehead, Anthony Ritchie, Chris Adams, Graeme Downes, Ross Carey, Pepe Becker, Claire Cowan and Mark Smythe – would each write a piece for harp. The whole sequence would eventually be recorded. (By the time of this interview in October, five have been completed and recording is planned for the New Year.)

When Helen returned from Dunedin she rang all her students.

'I said to them, "If you can make it over here to my house, I'll teach you. Any time." So I had pupils at 8.30 in the morning who came on their way to work. Never in my life

did I think I'd be teaching at that hour of the morning – but that was the only time they could manage.'

In July, after a four-month hiatus, the CSO once more settled into rehearsal, using school halls around the city and performing in the CBS Arena. And in October the orchestra went to Japan, performing first in Tokyo then travelling north to perform alongside the Sendai Philharmonic in its home town – the city that lay closest to the massive earthquake and tsunami that devastated that region of Japan in March. In Sendai the orchestras of two quake-affected cities combined to perform Tchaikovsky's 5th Symphony.

For Helen the experience of playing in Japan was simply amazing.

'We took the train to Sendai and on the way we actually passed through Fukushima station. Next morning some of the brass players went to the coast where the wave had

struck and played at a base there. When we flew out it was from Sendai airport, which had been inundated back in March, under six feet of water.'

But, says Helen, the most extraordinary thing was something that happened at the concert itself.

'The Tchaikovsky with both orchestras was just this big gorgeous thing. When we finished, the applause came. And then this Japanese woman came running down through the auditorium, up to podium where the chief conductor was standing. And she had this sign that she'd hand made – a big, big one. She handed it up to the conductor who held it up and it read: "BY POWER OF THE MUSIC WE WILL ADVANCE TOGETHER". She had drawn a New Zealand flag and a Japanese flag. Afterwards at the reception her sign was hung up as a banner backgrounding the speeches.'

'By power of the music we will advance together.'

Exactly.

Siene de Vries

'It was right under our feet: a massive upward kick that exploded all the windows and tipped everything from the shelves.'

Siene de Vries is an artist and sculptor who lives with his wife, artist and printmaker Saskia van Voorn, on a smallholding high above Le Bons Bay on Banks Peninsula. The two met when studying at the Academy Minerva in the Dutch city of Groningen. Together they lived on an old sailing barge moored on the banks of the meandering river Het Hoornse diep, on a stretch of river favoured by boat-dwelling students and artists.

They transformed the hold into twin studios. In 1981 when they graduated from art school they moved to an old farmhouse where they established themselves as artists, and their two sons, Tjalling and Wybren, were born. In 1988, in the wake of Chernobyl and the nuclear cloud that drifted across Europe, they emigrated to New Zealand, hoping to find here a safer and cleaner environment. At first they moved to

Nelson, where they stayed long enough to become close friends with local identity Eelco Boswijk. It is Siene's bust of Eelco that stands outside the iconic café Chez Eelco at the top of Trafalgar Street near the cathedral steps.

But the beauty of Banks Peninsula finally drew them south, to this place where we sit late one September afternoon, the sun setting across the valley on the massive rocky bulk of Panama Rock, a volcanic plug breaking a rugged skyline above regenerating bush. Siene is lithe, with the strong, capable hands of sculptor and farmer. He has just come in from milking. The house cow gave birth that morning and he has taken some colostrum for the freezer, in case other calves have need of a boost later in the season.

Saskia's 17th-century Dutch loom occupies part of the room, an inheritance transported here when they came in search of a place where they could paint, sculpt,

run a few cows and sheep, live a peaceful and productive life and raise their two little boys far from nuclear threat. The walls of the living room are lined with their paintings. He works in oils; she makes woodblock prints using subtly tinted printing inks. Plaster busts stand on a shelf in an old wooden press, one of them being of their son Tjalling, who is also an artist, in his Master's year at Ilam. We talk at the kitchen table, with coffee and cake.

On February 22 Siene was not here on the peninsula but in town. A trip to Christchurch, 100km away, means fitting in as many chores as possible. That day included a dental appointment, then over to Linwood High School to pick up a slate. As a fund-raiser the school was commissioning local artists to create artworks using slates that had fallen on September 4 from buildings about the city. Later in the day he planned to call in to visit Tjalling at his central-city flat, to leave

some milk and vegetables from the farm. With his slate in the back of the car, around midday he decided to head across town to visit a sculptor friend at Mt Pleasant. He had barely arrived when the quake hit.

'It wasn't like the other one, the September one. That rolled us about out at Le Bons Bay and felt like it came from a distance, but this one felt as if it was right under our feet: a massive upward kick that exploded all the windows and tipped everything from the shelves. I ran out and got knocked sideways by the door. Outside, people were screaming or calling out to one another, and a rock the size of a small car had rolled down into a ditch at the side of the road. I was thinking of Tjalling, who was taking down an exhibition at SOFA.'

The School of Fine Arts gallery was in the Arts Centre, a Victorian complex in the central city originally built to house the

province's university. It had been constructed with due reverence in the Gothic style of ancient English colleges: quadrangles and arches of heavy blocks of black peninsula basalt, trimmed with white limestone.

'Not a good place to be,' says Siene, 'in an earthquake.'

From Mt Pleasant he could look towards the city where a dense cloud was rising, and all he wanted to do was to find his son. To make sure he was safe. He tried ringing him. Repeatedly. He tried ringing Saskia, on her own at home here at Le Bons Bay. There was no answer. So he got in the car and headed toward the centre.

The road from Mt Pleasant follows the coast. It is narrow, only two lanes wide and it had become in an instant crammed with cars, as everyone else set off too, to find the people they loved: sons, daughters, partners, parents. On the car radio Siene learned of destruction in the central city, people killed in Cashel Mall, the collapse of buildings.

Back in September Tjalling's former flat had crashed down in ruins. It was an old mercantile building on Montreal Street. He had chosen it partly because it had huge bare walls where he could hang his work. Tjalling

is tall, and paints massive canvases. He needs a big space. The frontage had fallen away, the roof collapsed, bricks all over the road. He had survived then only because he'd been staying at his girlfriend's place that night.

In dense traffic Siene inched along the coast road until everyone was brought to a stop: the bridge across the Heathcote estuary was no longer passable. He turned off onto a side road, hoping to find a way through further up the hill, but rocks were tumbling from the tops. Volcanic boulders originally deposited millennia ago bounced on random courses down the steep hillsides.

'Someone stopped me and said, "You can't go up that way, mate." Everything was moving. Every few minutes there was an aftershock. People were out of their houses, on the road. Stunned, with big eyes. So I turned around, tried another route around the estuary.'

Winding through suburban streets, dodging rubble, circling back when roads were blocked by fallen buildings, he edged toward the city. About an hour and a half later he reached Colombo Street, where the traffic was completely gridlocked. The car radio had been broadcasting requests that people not use their cellphones as the system was overloaded. Siene found himself near the home of an elderly couple he knew well: some years earlier he had painted their portrait. They

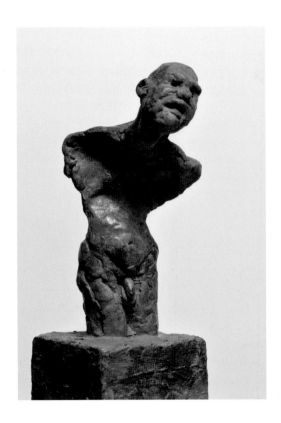

were in their house, shaken but unharmed
and waiting to go and stay with a son. Using
their landline phone he was finally able to call
Saskia and found that she too was safe out at
Le Bons Bay.

Back on the road again Siene inched
across town through traffic so dense that
eventually he decided it would be quicker
to walk. He would go to his younger son,
Wybren's, flat in Hoon Hay and pick up a
bicycle. Wybren was away, but his bike was
there: a BMX. Siene didn't bother making
any adjustments for size.

'There was a woman at the flat and she
said, "There are other bikes! Take a bigger
one," but I didn't care which bloody bike I

got. I borrowed a helmet too. A black one, one of those pudding ones.'

In the black helmet, knees up by his shoulders (he demonstrates, seated on the kitchen chair, his long legs making circles high in the air), he set off into the central city.

Tjalling meanwhile had escaped from the gallery, scrambling over rubble as the old university observatory tower collapsed. He was sitting out on the road with some friends when he looked up and saw – in his own words as he described it later – 'an old dude' pedalling towards him out of the dense dust cloud.

'An old dude on a bike. And I thought, "That guy looks like a looter!" '

The old dude was covered in dust and was pedalling for all he was worth on a small bike.

And then Tjalling took a closer look.

'That's not an old dude,' he said. 'That's my dad!'

We sit in the kitchen as the sun goes down and darkness sweeps up Le Bons Bay over the farms and bush-clad hills and Panama Rock. Siene talks slowly about his journey across Christchurch, taking care to be precise, using his capable hands to illustrate the story. The words take on some of the quality of a legend: one of those old tales where a father sets out to find his son and overcomes all obstacles placed in his path. I ask him as we come to the end of the conversation how it has felt, this past year of quakes and shocks. How has it affected him? Has it influenced his work, for instance?

Siene doesn't want to 'make sculptures out of piles of bricks'. It is the human drama that

has had a major impact on him, as it has on Saskia, and at some stage perhaps that might lead to art. Before the quake he had made a small sculpture called *Broken*, which might perhaps provide a model for work influenced by the dramatic events of this year.

'Funny things stick in your mind. Like this old man and his trailer. Just before the February quake I was looking for a trailer on Trade Me and there was one I thought would do. I'd been in touch with the seller and made an offer. After February 22 I rang and the seller – an old guy – said, "No, it's not for sale any more." His house had gone and all his belongings were now on that trailer and he was living in a van at his daughter's place, which was also in a mess. That has definitely stuck in my mind.'

But really, he says, the worst thing this past year wasn't the Canterbury quakes or the thousands of aftershocks. The worst thing was the quake several thousand kilometres away in Fukushima, two weeks after Christchurch was hit.

'Our younger son Wybren was in Japan – in the mountains on Hokkaido but near enough. We could go in to Christchurch after this quake to help, but that quake was so far away, *he* was so far away, and there was nothing we could do.'

Saskia nods in agreement. Yes. Wybren returned home safely, but that quake and its consequent nuclear risk felt worse, much worse, than the quake that was happening here, beneath their feet.

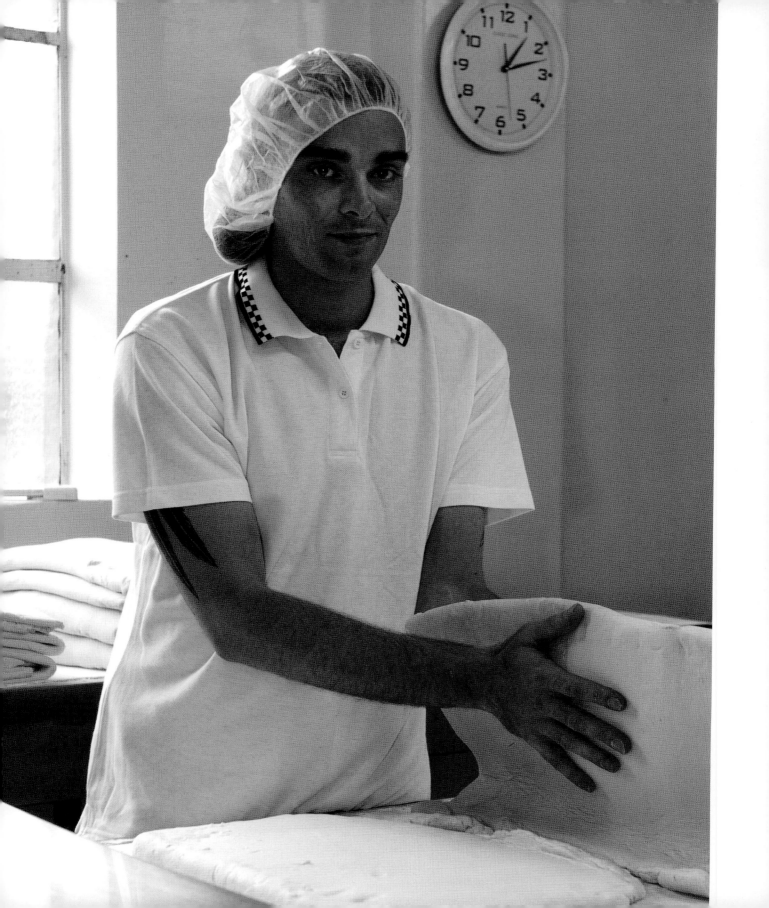

'The whole building started jumping up and down.'

Jaimini Shurety

There was a photograph taken on the afternoon of February 22 that haunts everyone who sees it. Two men seated on a low bench, cradling a third who lies across them, eyes closed, his face streaked with dirt. His arm is raised so that his hand rests against the tattooed arm of one of the seated men. The tattoo looks like bird's feathers and the man is wearing a chef's bandanna and checked trousers. He has his hands pressed against the injured man's sunken chest. The two seated men regard the camera with exactly the same expression of stunned incomprehension one sees on the faces of soldiers in World War I trenches.

When the photo appeared in the *Press* the caption read, 'Just after the quake, Tom Brittenden, right, and another man try to help injured baker Shane Tomlin, who later died.'

The 'other man' was Jaimini Shurety.

Today he works as a baker in a gluten-free bakery. His partner, Katie O'Neill, is in IT at the central library. They live in a villa on Armagh Street, along with two dogs: a Jack Russell/staffie cross called Piglet and a chihuahua called Kaylee. And two cats. And a canary. And two chickens and four rabbits, one of whom hops casually out the front door as we sit talking one Saturday afternoon in the sun on the verandah.

When I first arrived to talk to Jaimini, he and Katie were still asleep. Katie had given him Battlefield 3 for his birthday: it had only come out that week and they'd been putting in some late nights, tracking down stolen nukes on the Iran–Iraq border in the company of Sergeant 'Black' Blackburn.

The dogs race down the hall barking and Katie takes them out for a brief walk while Jai rolls a cigarette and we begin to talk.

In September 2010 he was working at the Trocadero bakery on Cashel Mall. He wasn't

trained specifically as a chef, though he had cooked all his life, taught by mother and grandmother.

'I was always asking them, "How do you do that? Can I have a turn?" They taught me how to make scones, queen pudding, just cooking with what you've got. One night a week – usually a Sunday – I'd cook for everyone.'

It was Jai's second year at the Trocadero and they were just beginning to gear up for Christmas.

'Christmas starts early when you're a baker: long before the jingles start. Christmas and Easter: they're the two busy times. Hot cross buns at Easter, cakes and mince pies at Christmas. You have to make a start three months out, look out the tins that have been kept in storage, make up the fruit mince. It's a lot of extra work on top of what you do already.'

What Jaimini did already, on a daily basis, was pastry: hundreds of sausage rolls, pies and bacon and egg slice. He worked in the bakery above the shop.

'The shop was small but there was a whole floor upstairs. It was quite a big place.'

There were three of them there: 'Me and Shane and Beverley.'

Jai's shift was from noon to 8pm, with Friday and Saturday off. The bread shift followed, working overnight 9pm–6am. Jai's done that shift too: 'It takes a bit of a toll.'

On the morning of September 4, a Saturday, Jai was asleep in their former flat in Weston Road when Katie suddenly smacked him on the chest to waken him and he became aware of a low rumbling sound, 'like one of your neighbours had left the bass on their stereo'.

That house was relatively new. Its chimney broke but did not fall and there was little

Katie had given him Battlefield 3 for his birthday.

damage. The only thing to smash was a bottle of teriyaki marinade. 'A full bottle I'd been keeping to use for something. I'd have been more upset if it'd been my flash vinegar.'

They texted friends and family, checked on elderly neighbours then went back to bed. That morning they went for a drive around the city, saw the fire that had broken out upstairs from Herbal Heaven just behind the cathedral, got some gas for the barbecue, checked on Jai's father, whose house had split, opening up gaps big enough to slip your arm through. (A year later he is still living there. The gaps have yet to be repaired.) They helped a friend move his stuff from a flat above a tombstone maker's in Colombo Street where a wall had collapsed, and he came to stay for a few weeks.

The Trocadero had not sustained much damage. Engineers had identified some risk from the brick wall of the taller three-storey building next door, but two weeks after the quake the bakery was deemed safe enough to reopen for business. The library, too, reopened and Jai and Katie's lives resumed.

The Boxing Day quake had little impact. They were in Akaroa visiting Katie's 99-year-old grandfather and on their return to the city noticed only minor changes. 'Some big ads down on buildings, and Wendy's had closed. There'd been all these ads for it on TV and we'd wanted to try it, but they were shut practically before they'd opened.'

On Tuesday, February 22, Jai was at work as usual.

'Shane would have got there around 10 or 11. He was always early. He'd always turn up to help the girls with shop things. I'd get there early too, but he'd usually be there before me.'

At midday, upstairs in the bakery, they were an hour into the daily routine, making

sausage rolls. Pastry was rolled out on two long stainless steel tables, each measuring around 2.5 metres. The tables were pushed together and he and Shane stood across from each other, rolling the pastry from one end to the other and from side to side. When it was thin enough it would be cut into four strips and sausage meat would be piped along each length: 300–400 sausage rolls a day; some-times, depending on demand, 600–800. The Trocadero, owned by a local family, supplied sausage rolls wholesale to schools, cafeterias and cafés all over the city as well as two shops downtown.

At 12.51pm the building started shaking.

'Shane was just across from me and we looked at each other. Was this going to get any worse? And then it did: the whole building started jumping up and down. Then everything failed. The power went out and all the shelves behind me started falling towards me so I shoved them out of the way with my hands. I didn't have time to look where Shane was. I just dived under the table in front of me. I couldn't have said anything to him anyway. It was way too loud. There was a lot of banging and then a beam fell on top of the table and split it in half.'

Big steel beams supported the building but the brick wall next door had fallen and a beam loosened and fell, hitting Jai in the ribs. 'All the air came out of me. Then the rumbling stopped and the air was full of dust. Black dust. Years of grotty flour and concrete and whatever was in the attic at that place. Hate to think. I couldn't see. I breathed in and managed to squeeze out from under the table. I just thought, "Right: get out of here – NOW!" '

He stood and as soon as he figured out he could still stand upright, he yelled for Shane.

'I put my hand out and found the table.

Straight into the sausage meat. Then I turned around to go to the door but I couldn't get through. All sorts of crap in the way. I had to go a long way round to get to the middle stairwell that goes down to the shop. I was still yelling for Shane. "Where are ya?" Climbed over the flour, over the racks. I was still yelling for Shane when I noticed the hole in the floor.'

Shane had obviously fallen through.

'I didn't go near the hole. I switched from yelling for Shane to yelling for Beverley and she was actually only about three metres from me around a corner. She didn't reply straight away. She'd got her handbag but she wasn't going anywhere. She said, "What happened to Shane?" And I told her and she said, "What are we going to do?" I said, "Let's just get outside." So I put my hands on her shoulders and walked with her down the stairs. We got down through the shop. It's

very narrow and the pie-warmer had fallen over so I shoved that out of the way. And the drink machines were by the door and blocking it. I squeezed through a gap under them and a builder helped me push them up so Beverley could get out. She said, "I can't get through there." There were all sorts of bottles and cans on the floor. But I said, 'Well, you have to." So she got out somehow. The girls from the shop were there outside in the mall, and the admin lady, Chrissie.'

Jai then turned back. He climbed across the mess into TS, the clothing shop next door, where he knew Shane must have fallen. He found him there, at the back of the shop, kneeling on a pile of rubble, 'with a nasty whack to the side of his jaw. I said, "Are you conscious?" And he said, "Yep." So I checked his arms, checked his body. Does this hurt? Does this? He said, "My back hurts." He couldn't move. All his ribs were clearly

The caption read, '…Tom Brittenden, right, and another man try to help injured baker Shane Tomlin, who later died.' The other man was Jaimini.

broken, and I couldn't move him on my own. So I went back outside to get help.'

Katie was there already. She had been at lunch at the library and she had run in bare feet over rubble and broken glass, straight to the Trocadero, remembering the cautions after the September quake and the risk from that neighbouring brick wall.

'I'd had one mouthful when the plate started moving. When I stood up I could see the old Government Buildings through the library windows and they were just a pile of stones.'

When she first arrived at Trocadero she could not see Jai anywhere.

Chrissie didn't recognise her and grabbed her by the shoulders.

' "Who are you looking for? You can't go in there." But I was in full fight or flight mode by then and ready to swing at her and go into the building when Jai suddenly

popped out from the clothing shop.'

Jai had noticed that 'some kayaking guys from a sports shop had run to their van and got their helmets and they were going from building to building down the mall checking on people. I ran down and said, "There's another person here!" They were getting someone else out, so while we waited I went in and out of TS to check on Shane, told him there was someone coming. I ducked back out when an aftershock hit, then dashed back in: "Are you all right? There'll be someone here soon." '

Out in Cashel Mall there was chaos.

'I remember this police officer: a tall guy, pale, who just looked at me and said, "What do we do?" I mean, you can train for it, but nothing can prepare you for that.'

A woman and child lay trapped under masonry.

'Some of us got a bit of wood and levered

the rubble away. The woman died as the stones were lifted from her, but the child – she was in a blue and white check uniform, primary age – she was still alive. Someone grabbed her and ran off to the hospital. I don't know what happened to her. Afterwards we checked the lists but there was no one that sounded like her. So maybe she survived.'

Bystanders covered the woman's body with a blanket of fabric from the clothing shop. The kayakers arrived, together with a St John's ambulance officer, and Jai led them to where Shane lay at the back of the store. Five of them gathered him up and somehow they managed to carry him out through the ruins.

They laid him on a bench under a tree.

'Shane was lying on top of me. Tom held his head. There was a doctor there and a nurse. They'd been somewhere nearby when it happened and they got a Stanley knife from one of the builders and cut off Shane's apron.

*His sister in Nelson rang the minute
she saw those tattooed feathers on the
evening news.*

Shane was still breathing but he was staring into space and not looking good. The doctor told me to place my hands on his chest so he had something to breathe against.'

Katie found a couple of T-shirts from a mannequin that had flown through a window and wiped Shane's face. Jai thinks they sat there for about three quarters of an hour, but he can't remember exactly. He does remember the photo being taken.

'I remember the camera being pointed at us, and the guy with a "Press" sign on his hard hat. He was taking a video. I remember it was like a war zone. There was an air force Hercules flying low over the city.'

Finally a police officer was able to back her car to the corner of the mall but it was too small to transport Shane in its back seat. They had to wait a little longer before a stationwagon made its way through and Shane could be carried on a stretcher improvised

from a piece of plywood, and placed carefully on its roof.

'The doctor led us; and the nurse, the police officer, the doctor and Tom supported the board as they drove to the hospital. They wound down the windows and perched in them and Tom stood on the towbar.'

There was nothing more Jai and Katie could do so they began the long walk home, through crowds of people, many with cameras.

'We said, "Don't go that way – people have died down there." And their faces changed and they turned around and walked the other way.'

It was only now, more than an hour later, that Jai began to feel his injuries. He doesn't remember feeling pain earlier, though in some of the photos he has his hand against his side so must have been feeling something. Along Papanui Road a 4WD pulled over and

a girl asked if anyone wanted a lift.

'These two women with briefcases hopped onto the tray. I said to Jai, "Do you want to ride?" but he said no. We were walking faster than them anyway.'

Part-way home Jai began to feel as if every breath was hurting. 'I was making a sound. There are categories of feeling pain and making a sound is 6 or 7, with 9 being passed out. We passed a doctor's surgery and they confirmed that I had two broken ribs.'

They continued walking and returned home to find little damage. Katie says that on the historic Black Map of Christchurch their area was shown as gravel, whereas her mother's house just down the road – which had a lot of liquefaction – was on sand.

That night the cameraman's photos appeared on television, including a closeup of three men in Cashel Mall, showing just Jaimini's arm with its distinctive tattoo. Jai has

a beautiful tattoo of a raven across his back, his favourite animal ever since he was 14 and saw them in the Tower of London. 'They are amazing animals. They can recognise 250 things – colours, shapes, words. My email ID is "ravenschyld".'

The bird's wing feathers spread over his upper arms. His sister in Nelson rang the minute she saw those tattooed feathers on the evening news. His father, too, came around immediately and Jai was able to tell him everything – 'The best thing I've done' – as a means of coming to terms with what happened that day.

Shane died in hospital that night of his injuries, though amid the appalling clamour he was not identified immediately, causing great grief to family and friends. No one knew where he was, nor what had happened to him, for several days.

'A nurse said later that she had been

Jai still often uses the present tense when talking about Shane.

yelling at him to stay awake and he'd said, "Stop yelling!" He hated raised voices. He's a shy man. He'd have hated being on front of the newspapers.'

Jai and Katie did not attend his funeral. Instead, in March when it reopened, they went to KFC: Shane's favourite.

'He always collected the coupons – couldn't wait, went there after work, always saved a bit of chicken for Mrs Turtle. He loves turtles. He always had a Mrs Turtle.'

It felt like the right way to remember a friend.

Now, six months later, Jai still often uses the present tense when talking about Shane – 'He's a shy man', as if he were still alive.

He and Katie are back at work. Jai had some weeks of recovery to begin with, while Katie and other library staff assisted Civil Defence, setting up computer support systems for the repair of sewers and water mains.

As soon as Jai was mobile enough he gave Katie a hand, transporting computers and cabling from the library to the emergency headquarters in the Christchurch Art Gallery. On one trip they happened to glance into the library lunchroom: Katie's lunch from February 22 still lay, untouched, on the table.

The Trocadero's owner did not contact Jai directly, but Chrissie ensured that payment was made to replace things like Jai's good boots and his wallet and cellphone, which had remained in his work locker. A few days after the quake the head chef at the Italian restaurant on Papanui Road rang and asked if Jai would like a job. Sometimes at the restaurant Jai saw the detective who interviewed him after Shane's death.

'They came to see all of us who had been at the Trocadero very soon, before they moved on to the investigation into the Pyne Gould building, which was much larger and

going to be more complex. The detective used to come into the restaurant quite often. His wife was pregnant and would send him round for pizza.'

Have the quakes changed their lives? Well, they don't plan to move from Christchurch: 'Not on account of earthquakes,' says Katie. 'Not unless we win Lotto and can buy a lifestyle block.'

But some things have changed. Little things. Katie has a new tattoo. Because of what happened to Shane and the confusion over his identification at the hospital, she now wears her ID tattooed on one hip.

Full name: O'Neill, Kate Frances. Date of birth. Blood group. On a tattooed dogtag hanging from a tattooed safety pin.

Little things, like last night when they were playing Battlefield 3.

'It's online so you're playing other people, but there's also Campaign Mode which is more like a traditional computer game. You're a Marine and you're in Teheran and there's earthquakes going on. And we both sat back and said, "Shit, that's a bit close to home." You notice a bit more because you know what it's really like. We said, "If there's been a quake, why are the lights still going? Why is the power still on?" And there's one point in the game when you're standing on the back of a technical, a ute with a machine-gun, holding off these Russian soldiers, and an earthquake hits and you get thrown off the truck and a building falls over and hits a helicopter on the way down in a very movie-style scenario, and the hero gets buried underneath, and you think, "Mate, you're not going to be climbing out of that yourself!" But he does.

'And we both just said, "No way!" '

Jenny Glue

Not many paintings hang on the walls of Jenny Glue's rented house on Opoho Road in Dunedin. Landlords are particular about such things, not wanting holes in their precious gib board. Framed paintings are stacked instead, 10 deep in the hallway. But in the living room there hang two portraits: husband and wife. She in beautiful moss-green velvet, he in legal robe and powdered wig – for he is Alfred Hanlon KC, the famous advocate who dominated the criminal courtrooms of New Zealand for over 50 years with his 'commanding presence, brilliant grasp of facts, rich and expressive vocabulary and perfect courtesy'. He and Mary Ann were Jenny's great-grandparents.

In an odd way it is also due to Hanlon that Jenny met her husband, Mervyn. In 1985 Television New Zealand made a drama series about his more spectacular cases. Jenny, who was an actress, had a minor role and one afternoon at Avalon she met another of the actors. She was chatting with her director at the time, who asked her, teasing, why she was still single. She shrugged. 'Where are the men?' From across the table came a hopeful voice: 'Here I am!'

Jenny tells me the story in her rich contralto, laughing at the memory.

We are talking late one afternoon. She has already been along North East Valley to Ross Home, where Mervyn is in the hospital wing. He was evacuated from Christchurch to Dunedin on the evening of February 22nd when several retirement homes across the city had to move their charges at quick notice to homes and hospitals around the country. They were swiftly transported to places that had power and water and the facilities for proper care.

In September 2010 Hanlon and Mary

Anne and all the other paintings stacked in the hallway in Opoho hung about the walls of Jenny's home of 25 years. An Edwardian villa in Christchurch's Avon Loop, it overlooked the river and was filled with family treasures and the mementos of a long and busy life. The Loop was 'a warm and friendly community'. Each day between 10.30am and 1pm she visited Mervyn at the Churchill Hospital in Richmond. She was also assisting her daughter and grandchildren through a fraught separation. One of her sons was living at home and studying law at Canterbury University, while other children lived nearby in St Albans and around the corner in Hurley Street.

Christchurch was home, though Jenny had been born and raised in Dunedin.

'I left home when I was 21, went to Wellington, became a kindergarten teacher, married and had five children, divorced, and at 50 I met Mervyn.'

Mervyn Glue, known to legal colleagues as 'Sticky' – what else? – was a barrister specialising in criminal law, a man recalled with enormous affection at his retirement in 2006 at the grand age of 80; a man who was prepared to represent people unable to pay, back in the 1960s before legal aid was abundant; a man generous with his assistance to young lawyers entering the profession. Mervyn was also an actor, a protégée of Dame Ngaio Marsh, and appeared frequently on stage and in films and television.

'This man had very blue eyes, and he kept staring at me. So you could say we met across the casting couch at Avalon.'

Five months after that meeting they married, and though Mervyn offered to shift his practice from Christchurch to Wellington, they decided to make their lives together in the south.

He asked her why she was still single. She shrugged. 'Where are the men?' From across the table came a hopeful voice: 'Here I am!'

The house in the Loop amply accommodated them all.

'I loved the Avon flowing past. Loved the area. It was close to town, you could walk to everything, yet the Loop was so peaceful. It didn't feel like inner city at all. I felt so safe and happy living there. People lived their own lives but there was this little community. There was a warm enthusiasm. People cared about all sorts of issues.'

The state of the river, for example. It had changed noticeably. When Jenny first arrived in the area the riverbed was shingle and the water ran clear. Twenty-five years later the water was murky and the shingle had completely disappeared under a layer of filthy mud. On September 3 there had been a meeting about this with a city councillor.

'Right at the end someone actually asked him, "If there's an earthquake, what has the council got in place for suburbs like ours?"

And the answer came back: absolutely nothing!'

The next morning Jenny was shaken from sleep. Her son, daughter and grandchildren were sleeping in other rooms but she could not go to them as the villa was swaying so violently. When it settled she suggested coffee, to calm everyone down.

'But there was no water of course, and no power. So we ferreted around for some torches and candles and matches and then we all sat on the sofa cuddling the children and trying to make something so abnormal feel normal.'

Her grandson – only six – said, 'Ooh, that giant was clapping his hands!'

There was damage of course – broken china, books tumbled from shelves – but the house itself appeared to have suffered relatively minor structural disturbance.

'The fire brigade came round at the

end of their shift at 7pm and took the two chimneys down and covered the holes with tarp. They were so kind. They also told me they'd just been to an old man and found him sitting up in his bed with fallen bricks in a great mound on either side. But really, after that quake, our house seemed repairable.'

In February all that changed.

'I had just been to visit Mervyn and on the way home I decided to stop and pick up a few things at the New World on Stanmore Road. That was where I was when the quake struck.'

It was terrifying. She remembers the things she had in her hand, and that out in the carpark she found a neighbour draped across her car whom she assumed at first must be dead. But she raised her head, much to Jenny's relief. Jenny also remembers that she hadn't collected her change.

'New World's still got that!' she says,

laughing her rich warm laugh at the absurdity of such trivial recollection.

In retrospect she cannot understand why she then decided to drive with her neighbour the relatively short distance between the supermarket and home rather than make her way on foot.

'It took three hours, winding through side streets, avoiding holes and cracks and the heavy, heavy traffic. Everyone else was panicking too: people were sitting on fences screaming, water was pouring everywhere, sewers were broken. We eventually abandoned the car. It was futile.'

There was another pressure.

'We were both desperate to use a loo by this time and this very sweet Maori girl let us come into her house and use hers. Her whole place was wrecked. A complete ruin.'

At last Jenny arrived back home in the Loop, where she received word that Mervyn, along with other patients from Churchill Hospital, was on an air force plane on his way to Dunedin. She cannot now remember who contacted her or how they did so, but the news meant that immediately, wearing the clothes she stood up in, she raced down with her son to Dunedin to check that he was all right.

'At first we didn't know where he was, but eventually we found him at Leslie Grove Rest Home. They'd arrived there at 11.30 at night, absolutely frozen. Of course air force planes aren't heated – and there were other problems: not enough wheelchairs and so on – but the quick evacuation was the best thing they could do. Some of the hospital board had visited New Orleans in the aftermath of Hurricane Katrina and discovered that the old and infirm were simply left behind. They were determined not to repeat that in Christchurch. So full marks to them!'

This whole episode is something of a blur now. Jenny recalls confusion as caregivers grappled with the problems of unexpected arrivals and new medications. The Red Cross paid for Jenny's accommodation at a motel, but as days stretched to weeks it became clear that some longer-term arrangement would be necessary.

'The motel owner mentioned that he managed a property in Opoho for an owner in Wellington and that it had become vacant. And it's perfect. Mervyn had been moved by then to a permanent bed at Ross Home, which is just along North East Valley. There is a supermarket half a block away; the Gardens are across the road.'

She has been here now for eight months. In that time she has been back to Christchurch only once.

'I went up to see *The Importance of Being Earnest*. I was supposed to be playing Lady Bracknell for David Sheard.'

It's a part she adores and has done before. She has been acting since she was 15: a 60-year career largely spent in amateur dramatics during which she has played everything from Lady Macbeth and Madam Ravneskaya to the hapless Linda opposite Mervyn's Willie Loman in *Death of a Salesman*.

'Ah,' she says, 'the dear old Repertory! The Hall of Radiant Living!' (The Repertory Theatre occupied a hall on Armagh Street originally built by Thomas Edmond, the baking powder manufacturer, to house the devotees of an American spiritualist movement that had many followers in 1920s Christchurch, including his wife. A pretty building in the Spanish mission style, it was in the process of being renovated when the quake brought it down in ruins.)

'David Sheard had started his own company and I'd done a reading for him – an

Alan Bennett. He'd carried on after the September quake, doing things in a tent at Deans Bush. Elsie Edgerton-Till had taken on Lady Bracknell and I thought it would be nice to go up and see her.'

She also wanted to try to locate old friends: difficult, because so many had moved away. She wanted to check on her house, where her son continued living, despite the fact that the entire Avon Loop is orange-stickered and will quite possibly see multiple demolitions.

Already 13 flats, built only 15 years ago next door to the Glues' house, have been pulled down. The insurance company suggested that someone should stay in the house as often as possible as there has been a lot of looting in the area.

Jenny has not been back to Christchurch since that visit to see *The Importance of Being Earnest*.

'I feel split in two,' she says. 'Half of me is here in Dunedin. I have to be here, because Mervyn is here and I can't move him again. And half of me is in Christchurch, but as people move away, the threads there are getting thinner and thinner.'

Friends are uncertain, not sure whether to stay or leave. The Loop's fate hangs in the balance and will not be decided for months yet.

'We've been told we'll find out in three months' time. But in the meantime we're in limbo.'

So she has brought some of her paintings to Dunedin. Paintings by people she and Mervyn have known, like Trevor Moffat whose beautiful portrait of his father bending down to tie his boots as he dresses to go to war hangs in the living room. And a lovely Olivia Spencer Bower portrait that has found a place on the hall wall. She misses

'I put my hand on the sofa and it was sodden. The liquefaction had seeped through everything, rising up through the floorboards.'

so much that has been left behind: all their books and the theatre memorabilia collected by them both over the years; so much that had sentimental value and is now broken. A theatre director friend, Graeme Anderson, who died a few years ago, had inherited a collection of china from his mother, some of which he bequeathed to Jenny.

'I treasured those pieces,' says Jenny. 'Cups, saucers and plates, all numbered. She was a great collector. Spode. Worcester. It wasn't the value of them, it was because they reminded me of Graeme. He used to come and do my garden for me as well as directing at Repertory: he was the most amusing man.'

She remembers other things: cutlery, for instance. Her mother's silver, the pearl-handled fish knives, her mother and father's furniture. A beautiful bed, a chest of drawers, a desk. All left behind.

'But when I was up in Christchurch and

visited the house I put my hand on the sofa and it was sodden. Water just poured out. The liquefaction had seeped through everything, rising up through the floorboards.'

Until the insurance companies give her some definite answers and she knows whether the house is to be rebuilt or demolished, everything remains suspended.

Meanwhile she makes the best of things in Dunedin, looking up old friends and making new ones, visiting Mervyn each day, helping her daughter and grandchildren settle into their new lives. She thinks a good deal about Christchurch, and in particular how things might be done, post-quake.

There must be restrictions on the height of new buildings, she believes, so that those who work in them or visit them need not be fearful of entrapment in lifts or on broken stairs. There must be rigorous building standards applied in reconstruction. And why don't they seize the opportunity to reduce class sizes in the city's schools now that rolls are falling in some areas, instead of making teachers redundant?

'There needs to be a focus on compassionate things,' she says. And as she speaks there is in her voice an echo of her illustrious ancestor – that 'rich and expressive vocabulary', along with 'perfect courtesy'.

'When we had that quake in June something changed … People shut down. Their arms closed around their chests.'

Juliet Neill

The basement in Juliet Neill's house in Lyttelton is taken up with a large work table, paint pots, paper and all the clutter of materials required for making puppets. Their knobbly faces line the walls: Tex the geriatric cowboy, a bellowing operatic diva and a bevy of vicious ferrets. In one corner, slumped in a chair, is a life-size bag lady with wild hair and laddered stockings.

'That's Daphne,' says Juliet, and I feel as if I am being introduced and should say hello. Daphne says nothing in reply of course. She looks as if she's had a few too many gins for easy speech.

Daphne and the puppets are Juliet Neill's crew: with their assistance for the past 12 years she has been able to stage puppet shows. Each year at midsummer Daphne has staggered unevenly down the streets of Lyttelton as one of the characters in the annual summer street party. It's a wonder she has been able to make it home again afterwards, up the steep little streets of the port town where containers line the wharves and the cranes creak and clang all night long.

Juliet also stages murder mystery parties: writing the scripts, booking atmospheric venues, guiding groups of 21st-century New Zealanders into new roles as the passengers on a pre-war cruise ship, limping into Lyttelton Harbour complete with nefarious individuals with heavy German accents and a shocking knowledge of nuclear weaponry. Or a 1920s family squabbling in a grand country house over Grandpa Basil's will. Or a selection of medieval knights and ladies getting down and dirty with evil King John, whose benign exterior conceals a rapacious intention to raise taxes.

But today we're not in a country house wondering who was in the conservatory at 2am with a Lueger, but in a very pleasant,

sunny living room, c.2003, overlooking a busy port. The road outside winds uphill till it ends in manuka and regenerating bush beneath a dramatic serrated skyline: Lyttelton is a compact little grid of buildings on the inner slopes of an ancient volcano, its port a flooded caldera. From the living-room windows we can see the wide blue spread of the harbour surrounded by massive tawny hills with a sprinkling of houses on their lower reaches. We can also see the port with its ships, trains, containers and cranes. We can see more of it than was possible a few months ago, says Juliet, because so many of the buildings that used to line the front – Edwardian pubs (the British, the Royal, the Canterbury), mercantile buildings, fish and chip shops – have been demolished: damaged beyond repair when Lyttelton was flung into the air on February 22. An unsuspected fault-line lay beneath the town and its harbour.

The front now is a row of vacant plots.

'I could never see the port like that before,' says Juliet. 'I'd never have been able to see that train.'

Things have changed, and not just physically.

'In September and again in February people had their arms open. But when we had that quake in June something changed. Something intangible. People shut down. Their arms closed around their chests.'

She senses it when she visits the new 'pop-up' Lyttelton info centre.

'In February everyone had a purpose. Even the most dysfunctional people felt wanted and made themselves useful, but that's gone. We're not in a state of emergency any more; those people who can, have moved back to their little houses. There was a feeling of community empowerment here in Lyttel-ton. We thought we could come together and

be in charge of our own destiny, but that's become less and less: now it's all insurance and this massive faceless bureaucracy – it's just deadened everything.'

Back in September 2010 she was busy as usual, with her puppets and murder mysteries, gearing up for Christmas and its flurry of end-of-year functions. She was adapting scripts, taking bookings, arranging venues.

'The groups liked those big old houses around town – Eliza's Manor House, Newbury House in Opawa, Riccarton House – places where they could dress up in their costumes and have a bloody good time.'

What she recalls most about the first quake is how very, very cold she felt afterwards. 'I got up, went outside, checked on my neighbours, then I went back to bed. The power was out, and I just couldn't get warm. Shock, probably.'

The most difficult immediate problem

was getting news, without power or a transistor radio. 'Not remotely prepared!' She presumed the Alpine Fault had ruptured, as had long been predicted. It was not until the sun came up and she was able to walk into town that she learned about the Greendale Fault and what was happening across the city. 'I talked to people on the street, my neighbours – my lovely neighbours, who became my Quake Buddies.'

In the weeks that followed, somehow things recovered. Some of the venues she normally used had been damaged but they were repaired. In Lyttelton buildings were 'propped up' and only a few had to be closed or demolished. Personally, Juliet also felt as if she was on the way to recovery.

'The aftershocks were horrible, toxifying, releasing all that adrenalin into the system. But a capsule a day of St John's Wort did wonders. And the garden. I put in this

garden. It was spring and it just seemed such a positive thing to do: helping bring the broken ground to life.'

At Christmas she left Lyttelton for a road trip around the southern lakes with a friend from the West Coast.

'It was good to get away from the shaking, though I found people elsewhere thought we were being a bit over-dramatic at that stage, exaggerating things. But really it was like a near-death experience for me: your outlook on life changes. I can't describe exactly what the change is – and I know it can become obsessive and unhealthy. You can start to feed off it. I wasn't obsessive but it had been a major event in my life, and my friend didn't really want me to talk about it. She said, "Oh, I've felt earthquakes! Don't go on about it!" '

They saw the Boxing Day footage at HariHari. Juliet sat in front of the television feeling sick, for Christchurch and all the small businesses that had been shaken up again in the central city.

'I just said, "Oh, poor Christchurch!" And my friend came in while it was playing and I think that was when it really dawned on her that this was not an ordinary thing: there was something major going on here.'

Coming home from that trip was nevertheless 'like coming back to a family. You know how there are things in families that go unsaid, but are understood without the need for explanation? That's what it felt like, coming back to Lyttelton, where everyone knew what it had felt like, and understood.'

On February 22 Juliet was working on one of her mystery parties: a cruise ship scenario featuring the evil Hans Off and his compatriot Helmut Ohn.

'All very silly. I was at my computer working on the script when the world started to shake.'

In September nothing had fallen from shelves but the motion this time was more violent and vertical: 'what we now know as the trampoline effect.'

Juliet was not flung from her chair but chose to sit on the floor as everything crashed about her, inside and out.

'I watched the whole thing happening down there in the harbour. The water seemed to rise and there were stripes of brown in it, like blood vessels in a giant eye. And then there was a line of dust that rose all the way along the waterfront, and out on Quail Island there was another line of dust as the cliffs collapsed. Not many people saw that.'

Rumblings signalled the fall of rocks from the steep hillside above the town.

'At the top of this road there are a couple of houses that have been closed off or have had rocks through them. There are still rocks poised to fall if we have another major event: they don't know how to move them. They're too big and dangerous to deliberately dislodge.'

Juliet had a cup of coffee in one hand.

'I knew what was going to happen this time: the power would be off, the tunnel would be closed, the road to Sumner could be blocked by rockfall, we could well be stuck. I sat there thinking, "Don't spill this coffee! It could be the last you have to drink for a very long time!" I was determined to hold on to it.'

Still clutching her cup she went outside, 'crunching my way over the ancestral china and what remained of the grandfather clock'. It now stands in one corner, its head devoid of dial and workings, covered in a pillowcase. An antique dealer has visited to examine it and advise on restoration.

'There it was, the cabinet smashed to bits and I said, "If you're going to restore

it, could you restore it so it won't fall over like this if there is another quake?" And he said, "Well, yes, but it will destroy a lot of its value!" I thought that was a bit odd, given the circumstances.'

In the garden Juliet found her neighbour, who had managed to vault the fence between their properties. Together they set off to find Juliet's daughter Tessa, who had a flat down on the waterfront and worked at the Coffee Company on London Street.

'It took a long time to walk down. The road was rippling the whole time, power lines were smacking around. Periodically more dust would rise from some building and every time there was an aftershock we'd grab one another and hang on. There were crowds of shocked people everywhere and of course you know everyone in Lyttelton and they all wanted to stop and figure out what had happened for them and you. It took ages to get down.'

On London Street Tessa was safe. The stairwell at her work had collapsed but she had with difficulty been able to force open doors and escape. She was standing with 'the woman from the fish and chip shop: a gorgeous, vibrant person, the kind who made you want to go into the shop because she was there – she'd nearly been killed when the building came down and was in profound shock, and desperately worried about her children who were in the city, on the other side of the tunnel.'

Juliet accompanied her to the Recreation Centre on Winchester Street, where survivors – those shocked or injured, old people wrapped in blankets – were gathering. 'We were lucky in Lyttelton because the army was over here on some kind of exercise, so they immediately cordoned off dangerous buildings and they fed people, took care of them. They were amazing.'

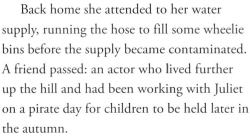

Back home she attended to her water supply, running the hose to fill some wheelie bins before the supply became contaminated. A friend passed: an actor who lived further up the hill and had been working with Juliet on a pirate day for children to be held later in the autumn.

'John said they were heading off to Little River and would I like him to text if they were able to get over Gebbies Pass? So I said yes, and as soon as I knew it was viable I drove to Little River to a friend's place to spend that first night. After that, I escaped to my brother's place in Queenstown.'

She stayed away two weeks. There was no point, she says, 'in a little old lady toughing it out, with no amenities, digging a hole in her garden for a toilet …'. Her house, amazingly, had suffered only minor damage and as soon as sewerage, water and power were restored she returned.

'What I remember from that is driving into Christchurch and the whole of Hornby being coated in dust. And opening the door here to the smell of fermenting soy sauce in the carpet and the smell of sewage, and the dust that was over everything in here too.'

Tessa came to help, and a neighbour whom Juliet had never previously met before knocked on the door to offer assistance. With their help Juliet tidied everything away, cleared the debris, took down what had not already fallen and stacked it all in cupboards and in the basement. There it all stayed for a few weeks until she could not stand the austerity any longer.

'I couldn't bear camping any more. Couldn't bear all these bare walls around me.'

She retrieved everything from storage and put it all back on the shelves and the walls, and she began work, preparing for the Festival of Lights that takes place every year

'*If you wear a denture, keep it by the bed. And always sleep in your pyjamas, just in case . . .*'

in Lyttelton at midwinter.

'It was planned for June 23rd. I made a phoenix puppet for it. It was going to rise from the ashes, or rather the rubble. I actually made rubble for it. Not many people have deliberately made rubble around here this year but I did! But that festival got quaked out on June 13th. So the phoenix sits in my basement, unrisen. And all my polystyrene rubble is in a friend's shed.'

They restaged the festival in July, but 'I didn't feel it was the right time for the phoenix. Not yet. Who knows what's going to happen? The aftershocks were still pretty bad. They had a wonderful delayed festival though: heaps of people came.'

Juliet returned to work on her murder mysteries. To begin with it was hard.

'One group wanted to do one only two weeks after the June 13 quake. I had to really force myself but I'm so glad I did. It was a work group, over 40 people, in the Riccarton Scout Den because Riccarton House was unusable: the medieval scenario. And it was the most wonderful, happy occasion. They were so funny! And I felt like I was giving all this pleasure to people, and that I had to hang on to that – that feeling of giving and receiving pure joy.'

Hanging on to that feeling of elation, though, is not easy.

'Sometimes I think going through an earthquake is a bit like having a little dalliance with manic depression: all your senses are so heightened. There's that constant swing swing swing from high to low all the time. I'd love to be able to hang on to the feeling I had that night at Riccarton. It felt like a kind of lesson. Something I learned.'

The other thing she has learned and wants to retain is the certainty of the kindness of strangers.

'People are just so kind. Once or twice when I was down south after the February quake I had these little meltdowns, and people were just gorgeous.'

In July she made a long-anticipated return visit to Flores, in Indonesia. It is a place she knows well. She has spent a lot of time in Indonesia and speaks the local language, Bahasa. In 1992 Flores experienced a massive quake in which 1500 people were killed.

'I met someone who had seen the Christchurch quake on satellite TV and he said, "When I saw footage of Christchurch, I cried. I cried for the people of Christchurch and I cried for us." When he was a boy he had hung on to his mother while everything rocked, killing most of his extended family. He said that that alertness to strange noises, unexpected bangs and so on has never left him.'

Are there any other lessons from this year of tectonic activity?

She pauses. Gives the question due consideration.

'If you wear a denture,' she says, 'keep it by the bed. And always sleep in your pyjamas, just in case you are compromised by the unexpected.'

So, down in the basement, next to Daphne with her wild hair and rakish hat, the phoenix waits. Fifteen metres of scarlet taffeta feathers, a massive papier-mâché head, wreathed in fire, requiring three puppeteers to operate. It's scheduled to rise in March 2012, at the Pirates of Corsair Bay festival for children and families.

Shiny gold and scarlet, from its pile of handmade rubble.

Diana Madgin

'People were so kind,
but I was numb.'

The garden on River Road is beautiful. A cherry in full pink blossom stands among beds of daffodils, blue matchsticks and scarlet tulips. Old fruit trees – black cherry, Bon Chretien pear and apple trees – flower in profusion. A massive walnut stands by the garage, its limbs still bare at the end of winter. Diana tells me it is one of many in the area that were planted as an avenue in 1888 when this part of Christchurch was still farmland. She loves such details of history, especially the history of plants and gardens. A film of grey liquefaction covered the garden only a few weeks ago, and an artesian well burst its pipe behind the little shed where for years Diana has written her articles about gardens and prepared the garden tours she conducts around the city and, on occasion, to China. Her partner, Bill Willmott, was born in Chengdu, the son of Canadian missionaries,

and links with China have remained strong.

Today the signs of flood and liquefaction are near invisible. They have vanished beneath lush spring growth.

Gardens have always been central to Diana's existence, ever since childhood on a rehab farm in Southland, helping her father harvest potatoes. She created her first garden when newly married, around a little state house where a neighbour handed bucketfuls of dead guppies across the fence for her to dig in to improve the soil. Writing about gardens came later, though its roots lay in childhood too, in the letters she wrote to relatives in England.

Her mother was English, a war bride. Diana wrote to aunts and cousins, in letters that became increasingly detailed. Years later when she first began travelling with Bill to China she wrote letters to friends at home. They were impressed by her evocation of

141

place. One suggested that she should write an article for *New Zealand Gardener*, so she did. It wasn't in fact about China, but about her daughter Katherine's first garden, created entirely of plants in pots.

'Things she'd found in second-hand shops. She bought a motley collection of bargain-bin plants and a large bag of potting mix and she made the tea while I potted them all up.'

One of those pots with its jaunty crew of tulips and jonquils stands today in the sunlight at the back door. The doors are open, letting in sunlight and air to this room where the walls are bare, the shelves stripped. Plywood covers the place where the chimney used to be, but the floor is stacked with cartons. Diana and Bill are in the process of moving back in.

In February they left in a rush. The ground beneath their home had buckled alarmingly and slumped. It had slid from its foundations leaving walls cracked, floors uneven and pipes burst. This leafy reach of the Avon River in Richmond was one of the worst affected by the lateral tectonic movement that does such damage to human structures. On the day the engineers declared the area zoned for demolition, friends rallied around. Within two hours they had packed away all the evidence of 35 busy years and taken it away for storage.

'People came from everywhere,' says Diana. 'A woman came off the street and said, "I was just walking along with my daughter and I want to help and all I can say is I am trustworthy." People were so kind, but I was numb. Everyone kept coming to me and saying, "Of these three things, which do you want kept? Which is the most valuable?" And I couldn't say. So everything was just stuffed anywhere. We found the computer

ages afterwards, under some boxes of tea, and my mother's ashes I finally found behind my sister-in-law's woodpile in her garage. I still don't know where everything is. We were so grateful to those people, but I can't even remember exactly who was here. It's a blur.'

In the midst of this chaos there was a phone call. A friend of her brother was offering them a house.

'My brother was a truck driver, and as a boy this fellow had adored trucks. He was always wanting to go off in the big truck with my brother. Now he himself drives buses for nine months of the year, taking tours around Australia, and while he and his wife were away their house in Hei Hei was going to be empty – fully furnished. So he thought he might offer it to someone. He was thumbing through his phone book when he came across my brother's number so he rang him and said, "Kruser," – my brother's name is Kruse

but everyone calls him Kruser – "I've got this house. Do you know anyone who might like to stay there?" And my brother said, "Well, yes, as a matter of fact I do." '

Diana and Bill shifted from their home on River Road to Hei Hei, on the other side of the city. It was a comfortable house: her brother's friend's offer was a lifesaver. But it simply wasn't home, and today Diana and Bill are moving back east. They have gathered up all those cartons, filled with books and china and tea and kitchen cutlery, and they are beginning the long process of putting things back on shelves and into cupboards. This won't be permanent. It can't be. The area is red-zoned. The house will inevitably be pulled down.

'We'll go eventually,' says Diana in her own sunny kitchen as Bill potters about opening cartons, exclaiming as he finds a book he likes, an object they'd been looking

for. 'But right now we need to say goodbye in our own time.'

The 1920s villa jiggles during aftershocks – but water flows from the taps, the toilet works, the power is on. It is possible still to live here. And most of all, the sun pours through the open doors, and the garden is beautiful.

And that is what we talk about: the garden, and others like it, built on the banks of the River Avon.

Diana has a project. She is a woman of great energy and right now her energies are directed toward preservation.

'Christchurch has always branded itself as "The Garden City", and I want to give the phrase real meaning. I want to preserve gardens.'

Her aim is to create a riverside precinct, reaching from the central city to the sea.

'The river marks a timeline,' she says. 'They are planning to demolish suburbs where liquefaction is inevitable and the ground has proved too unstable for building.

She is full of enthusiasm now, but her vision for a riverside garden route was born from despair.

They're thinking of wetlands and sports grounds – but there is an historical dimension to all this that hasn't been considered. I'm proposing a timeline along the river of heritage spots of houses and gardens that reflect the development of the city from Maori settlement to colonial settlement and on to the present. People could walk or cycle along the riverbank, or drive and walk down to the river. You'd start at Otautahi on the riverbank near the junction of Barbadoes Street and Oxford Terrace, which was an important Ngai Tahu collecting place for eels and fish. Their big gardens were out at Kaiapohia and Tuahiwi – 212 acres in wheat and potatoes and corn that were all ready for trade by the time the settlers came in 1850. But Otautahi was also a significant food-gathering place.'

She outlines a route past grand houses like Englefield, 'William Guise Britten's place, the first house in the borough of Linwood', built in 1852, and small houses like the cottages on Hanmer Street that were prefabricated in England and assembled in the colony. Visitors would then pass through the grounds of Avebury House, built in 1889, and so along River Road where a swathe of state houses was built between the wars with an expansive view of the river: solid houses, among the first constructed in the country for the workers in the new welfare state. The route would continue along the riverbank to this house with its gorgeous sunny garden and its neighbours, built immediately after World War I.

'The house next door had very little damage and we're hoping that it can be saved.' She quotes the Japanese architect Ryuki Miamoto, an expert on rebuilding in Japan's quake-damaged cities, who has visited Christchurch and criticised the rapid demolition of so many historic buildings,

DIANA MADGIN   145

insisting that many could be repaired and
made habitable.

'That house would become a café where
people could stop for a delicious coffee and
enjoy the gardens. Our own house will go,
so there'd be a big gap here, but it would be
a great spot for a community garden. Two
doors down there's another home with a
perfect traditional garden layout: currant
bushes and berries down one side, chooks
down the back. That house is scheduled to
be demolished too, but we could save the
garden. There simply aren't many left with
that plan that are completely intact. And we'd
work with the community gardens movement
to plant up the empty sites. Every autumn
at harvest time there might be cooking
classes showing people how to make jams
and preserves with the produce from these
gardens. It'd be a working model for school
parties, tourists, both local and from abroad.'

The route would continue to Kerrs Reach
where the river was straightened for rowing.
Here the houses are 1950s, '60s and '70s.

'Some will be lost but some will remain to
be pointed out as another architectural style,
and then people would arrive at that wonderful Anzac Bridge.' A bridge built, she says,
by 'my friend's daughter's boyfriend's father',
who had been contracted to dig piles to 35
metres but, finding no solid ground, insisted
(against some opposition from the council)
on constructing his bridge on piles 44 metres
deep. That caution paid off. The bridge
remains solid, providing safe passage over the
river, while all around on the sandy bed of
an ancient ocean that 6000 years ago washed
in as far as Montreal Street, more flimsy
constructions shuddered and fell. In the
future Diana is imagining, people could cross
that bridge and perhaps continue through
the wetlands the planners propose to reinstate

on the site of the failed '90s development experiment that was Bexley, to the estuary.

The conversation darts off into asides: the warmth of this neighbourhood and how they celebrated each New Year's Eve together. The creeks that used to crisscross Richmond before drainage, some so deep that a friend who was brought up in the suburb recalled standing as a boy in water up to his chest. The way old sandhills were levelled for building sites. The council's decision to replace 'The Garden City' with flashy new branding.

' "The City that Shines" – can you believe it? When I was conducting hundreds of Japanese tourists and journalists and others drawn to the city's reputation for fine gardens! I mean, what were those young marketeers *thinking*? You can't buy branding like that.'

She is full of enthusiasm now, but her vision for a riverside garden route was born from despair. 'I'd been talking to the city arborist about his plans for the green space they were proposing: I asked him how they planned to collect provenance for the lovely trees that exist here. And all he could say was, "It's the time of the bulldozers, Di. Maybe one of your little groups could collect

I cooked in the back yard and used water from the artesian well. I lived here on my own and I felt really strong.

provenance." ' ('Collecting provenance' means recording the stories attached to each tree. Who planted it? Why? When?)

The arborist's comment depressed her. And then, she says, 'I came out of it.' She wrote a piece for the *Press* about the loss of Christchurch's gardens, and from that came the idea for a heritage garden trail. Almost overnight a group formed, made up of landscape architects, community gardeners, heritage specialists and local historians. They set to developing the proposal, readying for encounter with the complex bureaucracy that has evolved to give shape to the post-quake city.

The year has taken a new and unexpected direction, since the house on River Road shook from its foundations. The September quake itself came as no surprise to Diana.

'We'd been out on a trip with the Royal Society some years before and the geologists were telling us about the Main Divide and the faults running under the plains and how tension builds and bursts at regular intervals, every 600 years or so. I remember standing there in the doorway when the shaking was going and I wasn't terrified. I was just thinking, "Well, the 600 years are up! That's all there is to it." It was one of my best moments, wasn't it, Bill?'

Bill agrees: it was. Diana was magnificently calm. She immediately got into her car and drove to check on her mother, who had just moved into a retirement home at Kerrs Reach.

'It was pitch black and there were these enormous holes in the road – you could easily dive into them. A huge crack opened up in front of me at one point but I just turned aside and kept going. And when I got there, there were all these old dears sitting with their emergency lighting, waiting to be

148   THE QUAKE YEAR

evacuated. Two days later, on the Monday, Bill was leading a delegation to China. He'd be away for two weeks. I just said, "Go! You can't do anything about all this. Just go!" '

Bill went as arranged, and her mother was evacuated to a retirement home in a more stable part of the city. Then, unexpectedly, Diana's daughter Katherine became acutely ill.

'That whole first week I was sitting by her bed as the hospital shook from side to side. The nurses, the staff, were amazing but it was seriously frightening. At night I went and slept at my sister-in-law's, but after a few days of that I thought, "Now, I've got to work out how I'm going to live with this! The hospital, the liquefaction, no power, no water, no sewerage." So I made a decision.'

She came home.

'I slept here. I used buckets and compost for sewage. I found a charcoal barbecue that was still in its box in the garage: the rats had nibbled the cardboard but inside it was still shiny – and I found an old singing kettle Mum had brought from the farm years ago. I cooked in the back yard and used water from the artesian well behind the shed. I lived here on my own and I felt really strong. Whenever there was an aftershock I worked out that I felt better if I just shouted at them: I yelled, and it felt as if I gained some power. They never lasted long anyway and I knew it was natural. I'd always been fascinated by geology and this was just geology. There was nothing to be frightened of.'

This calm carried her through the next months, which saw the death of her mother in her new and unfamiliar nursing home.

'Mum had been really rattled by the quakes. Between September and December she was shifted three times. She began having terrible panic attacks at all the dislocation.'

One night in December she got out of bed and, without her walker, fell and broke her hip. 'That was the end, really, for her. She died before Christmas.'

Two months later, in early February, Diana's younger daughter was visiting from the UK.

'She'd taken out everything she had stored in the attic and cupboards while she was away and spread it out to sort. Then this frigging earthquake happened. She was out driving along the river with Bill, and I sat there in all the mess, stuff everywhere, silt bubbling up out there in the garden again, and I thought, "Bugger it!" I had no idea what was happening in town: I had no power, no TV, no radio. At such times my inclination anyway is to go very quiet. I don't want TV or radio. I just want to be very calm and think what to do. All this liquefaction and sewage was running everywhere – over my books, over

my mother's stuff that I had stored in boxes out in the garage. So I put on my Crocs and thought, "Well, there's no point being squeamish. Half the world spend their lives walking through sewage!" So I waded in and started clearing what I could.'

A neighbour had been in the CTV building, at a meeting on the top floor. 'She'd somehow surfed down to street level as the building fell and got home at 5.30 looking as if she'd been in a war zone. We all had a meal together, supported one another.'

But that little community of friends and neighbours was about to disperse. The February quake rendered homes unliveable, the neighbourhood was red-zoned and Diana and Bill moved west to Hei Hei. Her days now frequently involved long hours in the car, dealing with new realities.

'Long, long lonely drives across town, just to get from A to B through a place that had

become somewhere we didn't really belong any more.'

It was during these long drives that Diana found herself attending to the real emotional impact of this past year. Those shocks have rattled more than buildings. They had changed everything within her.

'I felt exhausted, often shaky. And somehow the ground's shaking was mirrored in me. My established belief structures were shaken down by the quake. It shook to bits everything I am and everything I think. What happened changed me utterly.'

She found herself mourning her mother.

'Up until Christmas, when she died, I had been in survival mode: just clamping down, surviving the earthquake both physically and emotionally. But after February and the move out here, on those long drives I found myself talking to her.

'I had understood her reserve and

non-assertiveness as a British stiff upper lip. I
loved that reserve in books, but it was harder
in real life. After she died and the quakes kept
uncovering us, I realised she had had wonderful stuff to say. All those boxes that had been
my character were shaken down. I saw her
better, her deep loneliness. I was talking to
a friend whose mother is also old, about the
loneliness that one goes into with the frailty
of age. Somehow it's the essence of ageing: a
deep loneliness. You can have a busy life, with
whanau and connections, but regularly you
come up against that loneliness.

'That's what I dropped into while I was
driving around the city. Miles and miles,
day after day I was coming to a house where
I'd be safe and warm, but there was nothing
beyond that. I was going away from the river
and the community on the river. That whole
notion of whanau is so in the middle of me.
I'd always rejected that part of my mother

that didn't do that, but there it was: loneliness.

'I couldn't tell Mum these things. Our
time between September and December was
taken up with her panic at dislocation as she
was moved yet again, and her asthma, and
her fear of death.

'I'm scared of death too, and it was
hard in those three months, taking her out,
distracting her. She loved the sea, or along the
river. She loved the water, she found it really
consoling … sometimes we'd go out twice a
day.'

The rattling of the quake had stirred
everything up: Diana's perception of the
world, her isolation, her 'own deep emotional
poetic self'.

'I suddenly could see the world as a
continuum. It's all evolving, with a very
thin skin – so very, very fragile. I've always
thought this, but it was really crystallised

for me this year. We use all these words: "pre-Maori", "pre-European", "European", but what ridiculous words they are! I sat at a meeting listening to a mihi the other night, and suddenly I really understood it. Suddenly I understood that everything is predicated on what has preceded it. People talk such crap about history not mattering, but it does! We go forward, in anything we do, with the acknowledgement of what went before. I suddenly understood that with a depth I had never experienced before.'

Bill is carefully placing books back on the shelves of the house on River Road with its rolling floors and damaged walls. They are back home, to say a proper goodbye to their lives here.

'I want to honour the history of these old places along here,' says Diana. 'I haven't known what to with the feeling of loss. It's not like a funeral but there is still this overwhelming grief. We needed to come back to this place, to the house, but more to this garden. I need to bring our life back, including plants that good friends potted up and took away for me. I need to have everything back, to sell anything we won't need any more on my own front lawn. We are coming back here to live. We'll patch it up, we'll sleep here. We'll reclaim it. It's my sanctuary. I can't move forward if I'm not here.'

Across the back fence a massive new home is in the process of demolition. Since the area was red-zoned, several neighbours have bought elsewhere and moved. Five stay on. It will be 15 months before they have to move from their homes. Meanwhile, 'we're going to live here over the beautiful part of the year and sort things out quietly.'

In this garden.

It is, Diana says, 'my bedrock'.

She is well aware of the irony of the term.

Whenever they visited someone for a coffee or lunch the boys would ask, 'Is this our new home?'

Pip Watson

I talk to Pip one sunny Saturday morning at her mother's bach at Takamatua. Her two oldest boys are off with their Granny Robby collecting seaweed for the garden from the foreshore at Duvauchelle. Nixon, who is nearly two, is having a nap. It's peaceful. Pip has a friend to visit who is about to get married. They are planning a hen night out here, the week before the wedding. Right now her partner, Mark, is off at the stag do at Ohau. The muddle of September 4 a year ago seems very far away and long ago.

'I froze when it hit – but Mark pretty much slept through. I actually had to wake him up,' says Pip. 'I just stood in the doorway of the kids' room and didn't know what to do.'

Mark's sister Jo was staying with them and somehow they managed to gather up the children between them and find their way downstairs and under the table in the dining area of their home in Sumner. The house, built in the 1980s and recently renovated throughout, stands on the hillside below Evans Pass. It was not long before friends began arriving, looking for safety. Sumner is largely built on a flat and narrow marine plain between steep cliffs, the remnants of two old volcanic flows. They feared the quake would trigger a tsunami that would sweep across the valley. Pip and Mark's home with its elevated situation provided a haven. The power came back on there after only 40 minutes so everyone was able to watch quake footage from elsewhere around the city on TV.

'The boys were sleepy and a bit frightened. Luka was certain a big monster had shaken our house, but we explained what had happened and he became really interested in it all. We could hear him explaining tectonic

plates and so on to the other kids.'

But really, the September quake had little impact on their lives. The house felt a little unstable afterwards, rolling with the aftershocks. Jo, who is sensitive to motion, experienced a kind of seasickness and threw up for several days. But for Pip they had an oddly exhilarating effect.

'I got a kind of adrenalin rush from them,' she says. 'I buzzed for about an hour after each one. I felt really alive. I'm not normally an adrenalin junkie, but you could almost say I was addicted to them. Some of my friends felt the same.'

But in February all that changed.

Pip was at home that day, with the two younger boys. She was expecting a couple of other children whom she cares for two or three times a week while their mother works. In the busy interval before they arrived she had to give her own children lunch and

then drive down to Sumner village to pick up bread and milk and put petrol in the car. Nixon was in his high-chair, Olly at the computer. Within a couple of seconds it was clear that this aftershock was really big.

'I don't know how I did it, but somehow I managed to pick up both the boys and jump under the table.'

From there they watched their kitchen break apart. Bifold doors onto the deck were warping and Pip, crouching there with her two sons, felt pure panic.

'Just absolute panic. I never thought I'd experience anything so violent. The house felt like it was moving in lots of different directions at the same time. It was like – well, like being in a washing machine on spin.'

Pip screamed, and within moments of the initial quake one of the neighbours heard and came over: a 15-year-old boy who got under the table too and helped hold the children.

A massive volcanic rock weighing at least 1.5 tonnes had bounced from the hillside above onto their deck.

'Then another neighbour, Nicci, arrived at the back door, which couldn't be opened. She had to break it to get in. She'd seen a boulder roll down and wedge itself between the spa on the deck and the wall of the house.'

A massive volcanic rock weighing at least 1.5 tonnes had bounced from the hillside above onto their deck. All over Sumner and the other suburbs built in the lee of the peninsula hills, rocks deposited millennia ago by ancient volcanoes had been shaken loose.

Luka was at school down on the flat, along with the neighbour's young son. Nicci drove down to fetch them. The teachers had done a good job of keeping their charges calm. They had previously practised a quake drill that involved taking the children up a track out of reach of tsunami – but the startling and completely unexpected rock falls made that dangerous and impractical.

Instead, the children were walked half a kilometre up the road to Van Asch College, which is on higher ground than Sumner School, where they waited for their parents to collect them.

'I didn't want to be inside the house. It felt as if it could fall to pieces any minute. So we went next door to Nicci's.'

Her sister-in-law Jo arrived. Her rented house near the beach, beneath the cliffs, was now surrounded by fallen rocks. Nicci's husband arrived home, having run across the Causeway from town. Pip's husband, Mark, however, was away doing vegetation monitoring for Environment Canterbury in the high country, where the quake had scarcely registered. It would be four hours before Pip was able to reach him by cellphone.

That fact – the two wildly different experiences of the actual shock – made a difference to the way she and Mark each responded in the days that followed.

'Mark's way of dealing with it was just to get on and clean up the house. He looked at the rock on the deck and said, "Crazy!" And I couldn't speak. We just couldn't communicate very well.'

Almost immediately their house was red-stickered. Hundreds of boulders remained up on the hillsides. Any aftershock could dislodge them, putting homes below at risk. The family had to find somewhere else to live, and so began weeks of shifting from one temporary home to another.

'We went out to Dad's at Bentwood Winery, then here to Takamatua for two weeks. Then we went to my friend Julianne's cottage at Wanaka, and after that to my friend Tom's parents' holiday house. All of them welcomed us with open arms. We even thought we might stay in Wanaka. We enrolled the kids in school there, but we

found we missed our friends here in Sumner. So we came back to housesit for someone who had gone to Queenstown.'

Over the next couple of months they lived in seven houses – until the boys began to ask whenever they visited someone for a coffee or lunch, 'Is this our new home?'

'We just couldn't figure out,' says Pip, 'what would make us happy again.'

They all just wanted 'to go home'.

So that is what they did. They returned to their house despite its red sticker, which they moved and stuck to the back door. They warned friends against visiting, but it felt good nevertheless to be back in their own place. Pip's panic receded. They had a builder look at the damage, who reported that it might possibly be repaired. They settled back into some semblance of normality – though they kept some children's toys packed in the car, just in case. They had

water, though drinking water came on a truck. They had no sewerage but a portaloo was close by. They had power. And friends had begun to move back to Sumner after the flight in February.

One day in June Pip was chatting to a friend, someone she hadn't seen since February 22. Luka was at school, Olly at playgroup, Nixon still asleep in his carseat in the car in the drive. Pip and her friend were on the deck, talking and having a cup of coffee when the ground gave a massive jolt.

'This was big. It was ferocious,' says Pip. The epicentre was only a few metres away, just down the road (Geonet maps the location of epicentres with extraordinary precision.) The ground was moving so fiercely that neither woman could move. The steps and the deck were rocking together and apart by about 40 centimetres or so, 'exactly as if they were breathing'. Pip and her friend

clung to the balustrade, fighting to stay upright. (Their arms were covered in bruises for days after.) The noise was deafening – of things breaking and tearing apart.

When it passed, however, Pip felt oddly calm.

'I knew what I had to do now. I knew about quakes. I said, "You okay?" to Karen, and she said, "I'm all right. Are you okay?" "Yes, I'm okay." '

In his carseat Nixon was still fast asleep.

This time the house was completely wrecked. Beams down, unsteady on broken piles, walls torn apart. That night Pip and

Mark and the boys stayed at a friend's place, where they 'drank too much, and after the kids were in bed I lost it. Threw bottles, just so angry. I was so sick of it all, so tired of hearing about it every night on the news. I mean, the rest of New Zealand must just hate us: "Oh no! Here we go again!" '

After June it was clear the family had to make some longer-term decisions. They found a house to rent on top of Clifton Hill, with a clause that says the tenancy can be terminated if the access road should become impassable.

'It's almost like everyone has done this great house swap: no one stays in their own house, but they feel safe renting someone else's.'

They have this house until Christmas. Then who knows? Their insurance rental allowance of $330 a week will have been used up. They have yet to hear if the ground

beneath their property is zoned red or green, whether their house can be repaired or rebuilt.

What has held Pip together through this stressful and unsettled year?

'Having three kids has helped,' she says. 'And a big family network and a great Mum and partner. And having this place at Taka-matua to go to when it got too hard.' She pauses. 'And wine,' she adds.

And what has changed for her?

'Well, that sound – the roar of the quake and the smashing – will always be with me: even now, when a door slams shut it makes the hairs on my arms rise. But I also feel quite excited about what comes next. I'm curious to find out what will rise from the rubble. Christchurch was always such a conservative town and now everything's changing: schools sharing premises, bars moving out to places like Garlands Road, things are being all

mixed up. And I think in the big scheme, it will be better. Even now, there are all these people working to make it okay: Civil Defence, city councillors, EQC assessors, all those people – they've been outstanding.'

Personally, she feels a profound change within herself.

'You change in so many different ways; financially things are different. I don't think I've ever been a particularly materialist person, but now I really do know that you have to enjoy what's in front of you. Living in a red-stickered situation for months, moving to 10 houses in 10 months, you know it's all out of your control. There is just no point getting worked up because there is nothing you can do about it. It's just that the earth has shifted, doing what it does. It's not personal. You've just got to make the best of things.'

This quake year has been, she says, her own personal 'e-pip-any'.

'We don't sell much over the internet. Good food needs to be bought face to face.'

Martin Aspinwall

Much of the central city is still fenced off as spring comes around and the trees break into leaf in Hagley Park. Buildings remain dusty and desolate behind netting and red tape, their former tenants resettled in the suburbs. But on a sunny Tuesday morning on Montreal Street at the edge of the CBD, one business has its doors open. The Cheesemongers has refurbished a ground-floor site at the Arts Centre.

The chill room is filled with rounds of Lancashire and Meyer Gouda and Evansdale, the smell of fresh bread fills the shop and there are little tables on the terrace. The view may take in stacks of fallen stone around the cracked Gothic walls of the former university, and the soundtrack may mingle music and birdsong with the noise of demolition and reconstruction. But the sun is out, there are people seated at the little tables reading the

paper and someone is whistling cheerfully over the drills and hammers, somewhere in the direction of the former Dux de Lux, behind the netting fence.

Martin Aspinwall says they have been lucky. He says it many times as he recalls this year, until it almost becomes a mantra.

'We've been lucky.'

He talks about luck, and earthquakes and making cheese.

For over a decade he has been a familiar figure around Christchurch, ever since he arrived in the city with his New Zealand-born wife, Sarah, in 1999. The two had met when working at the Neal's Yard Dairy in Covent Garden.

'I'd been a social worker in London but I'd always bought cheese from Neal's Yard. It's big now, with about 85 staff, but 20 years ago it was this little hippie place with 20 staff wearing white aprons and wellies, right in

the middle of all the fashion shops in central London. One day I went in and said, "Look: you're only going to get bigger, and I can do staff management things, draw up contracts. And in return, will you teach me about cheese?"

Cheesemaking was not something Martin had been brought up with. He was born in Barnsley where his father was a bookbinder – but his mother had been a butcher and his dad's mum was a grocer, so 'we always had good food on the table'. It was not until he went to Neal's Yard, however, that he thought seriously about the food we eat.

'Most people bought their food from supermarkets without knowing really where it came from. Neal's Yard Dairy was founded in 1979 as a bakery, health-food shop and a shop where you could buy yoghurt and soft cheese. There were still about a dozen small dairies in England producing local cheese, and Neal's Yard offered them a shop window in the middle of London where people were prepared to pay a little extra to buy proper cheese from specific makers.'

When Martin joined Neal's Yard he discovered a philosophy that emphasised the

personal element in food production.

'The culture was: You need to know where the cheese comes from. We'd go out in a van at the weekends and spend time with people like Ruth Kirkham, who made Lancashire cheese. They had 40 Friesian cows and her husband John milked them morning and night. The milk would go into the dairy to ripen overnight, and every morning, all year round – even on Christmas Day – Ruth would put on her pinny and a hat and go out and make cheese. She reminded me of my mum. Ruth would have been in her fifties and she'd learned how to make cheese from her mum – and there was nothing special about it. That's what I liked most about it. It was just *ordinary*. But the cheeses she made were like nothing I'd ever tasted before. They were *extraordinary*.'

Sarah, too, had come to work at Neal's Yard, as part of a year's OE in London. They met, fell in love and worked together for eight years, learning all they could before coming to Christchurch, keen to bring the style and philosophy of Neal's Yard to a new context – which was a challenge in a country that had traditionally made its cheese in factories.

'There were no Ruth Kirkhams, though there were some smaller producers around, often Dutch immigrants like the family who founded Karikaas. Since we've been here, though, there's been a change: there's Crescent Dairy goats' cheese near Kumeu, Neudorf sheep's milk cheese in Moutere, and others.'

Selling such food is also intensely personal.

'We don't sell much over the internet. Good food needs to be bought face to face. You need to ask questions like "Who made this?" "Where was it made?" "How old is

it?" And it's bought in small quantities, like bread. An everyday purchase.'

This was the culture that Martin and Sarah hoped to establish when they set up as Canterbury Cheesemongers back in 2000, sourcing cheese from English and French producers and from around New Zealand, storing it in a cooler on their back lawn to undergo that vital process of affinage – maturing – and selling it at weekend markets from a van. They had a little yellow Simca they had adapted with a chiller and a gas cylinder and califont for washing hands.

They found ready buyers and in 2002 felt sufficiently confident to consider leasing permanent premises. They rented a small shop on Salisbury Street, part of a block that also housed a furniture shop, a massage parlour and a hairdresser.

'We really liked it. It was a hundred years old and for 20-odd years in the 1960s it had been a print shop. There was still ink staining on the floor. It had history.'

That corner of the city became something of a food destination: there were cafés along Victoria Street, Vic's bakery just up the road, a fruiterer opened in a former gas station, a deli, a specialist butcher. On Saturday mornings the area filled with people browsing, having coffee, picking up a cheese, fruit, meat for weekend meals.

In spring 2010 Canterbury Cheesemongers was expanding its range to include raw-milk cheeses. A law change in 2009 now permitted the production and sale of cheese made from unpasteurised milk.

'The best cheeses are made from raw milk. They have the best flavour. It's a bit like *terroir* in winemaking. Raw-milk cheese is not necessarily stronger in flavour but it is more complex. The taste will stay in your mouth long after you've eaten it.'

They could finally import Appenzeller from Switzerland, Brie de Meaux, Gorwydd Caerphilly … And they were keenly looking forward to the time when they could stock raw-milk cheeses from New Zealand producers.

'No one in New Zealand was making unpasteurised cheese, but it's only a matter of time. It will be small makers – the young ones starting out using their own milk from a small herd. The bigger producers get their milk tankered in and as soon as you start moving milk through tankers and pumps, mixing different milk from different farms, you lose it. Cheesemaking is very hands on, it's slow: some cheeses take six months to a year to mature. It's hard to make a living. It doesn't yet have the prestige of winemaking.'

Business was good, but then early one morning in September the city jolted.

'Our shop was not actually much damaged by the quake and we hoped it could be sort of unstitched from the other buildings and left standing: like those places that were left in Europe after the war. There'd be this total dereliction all around but then you'd see this little building still standing. A little symbol of survival after the quake. But it wasn't to be.'

The landlord was insistent: the entire complex was to be demolished. Within a week Martin and Sarah received their eviction notice. The *Press* ran articles about their relationship with the landlord, and TV3 also covered it, as an example of a central-city business being treated peremptorily by a landlord.

'The *Press* was tremendous at the time, running articles about small businesses, telling the public where they were and how they could be contacted. But still, we had to move.'

'But the Arts Centre had given us this building which is lovely ... So you see: lucky, all the way round.'

And this, says Martin, is when they experienced their first stroke of luck.

'It didn't feel like it at the time, but as it turned out, if you were going to lose your building it was best to lose it in September because though there were a lot of buildings damaged, there were very few actually looking for new premises. The CBD was relatively unscathed, compared with the disaster in February.'

Their building was demolished in September. But only a week after the quake the Arts Centre management rang Martin and asked if Canterbury Cheesemongers would like to shift to their site, which was still relatively unscathed and still staging its regular weekend markets.

'They said if you don't have any luck with your landlord, there'd be space in the old Registry complex here.'

The complex had been built in the 1950s.

'It was a warren of low-ceilinged offices but we could see possibilities, and we really liked this corner. We signed a lease in October last year, began our refit and reopened on January 18.'

They had been nervous of moving and losing custom.

'It had taken us seven years to develop custom in Salisbury Street. People had gradually discovered us. They were coming in to buy cheese and bread. We were just starting to relax, thinking, "This is working!" So moving felt risky. People get into a routine. They might not follow us.'

In the event, in its new premises the Cheesemongers experienced their busiest time ever. The site was central, the market and CBD were still active, and for five weeks Martin, Sarah and their staff were run off their feet.

'We were lucky, you see. Our old landlord

had actually done us a favour, because the shop would have come down for certain in February, if we had stayed on. But the Arts Centre had given us this building which is lovely, and also strong: it was built to 60 per cent of code rather than the minimum 30 per cent, and there aren't many like it in the city. So you see: lucky, all the way round.'

Their luck extended to making a living during the four-month interval while their new store was fitted out.

'When we opened the original Salisbury Street shop we sold the van. There weren't farmers' markets back then: just the Riccarton Racecourse market, which was mainly bric a brac and plants, and the Arts Centre market, which was mostly crafts. Lyttelton hadn't started its farmers' market, nor had Riccarton House. So we took the plunge and opened the shop on Saturdays, and right away it was busy. We had sold the van to the

Fat Albert Smokehouse people in Fairlie. The morning after the quake they rang up and said, 'Would you like to borrow the van?' They knew we were going to be closed and they just offered it.'

Martin and Sarah had not yet been offered the Arts Centre building. Their shop, though relatively undamaged, was about to be demolished. They had insurance for stock, but the only stock that had been ruined was a single Windsor Blue Cheese that had tumbled into a drainage bucket. They had no business interruption insurance.

'We couldn't afford to muck about. We thought, "Well, we'll just move everything to our garage, we'll get a big refrigerated container and park it up our drive." We lived in Richmond, and in that quake we hadn't had much damage. We didn't let Food Safety know: they were busy, and anyway, we thought, "If they let us sell cheese in a field

at Riccarton Racecouse they're not going to be too concerned if we sell cheese from our garage." It had a sink so we could meet all the hygiene requirements. So by the end of that month we were selling cheese from home.'

They also got the van back on the road. It had not been used for a year except as a refrigerated trailer towed by the new owners' 4WD, so while the fittings were in workable shape, the engine needed some work. Another friend came to their aid.

'Tonto the barista at Vivace. As well as making great coffee, his main love is old French vehicles! He came around – he lives nearby – and he repaired the van. A fuel pump needed tweaking. And he did it for nothing, He wouldn't take any money.'

Another phone call came.

'Jamie from Riccarton Farmers' Market rang us up and asked if we'd like to sell cheese there. So by the end of September we were all set up: we'd gone into the shop and pulled everything out – light fittings, shelves, the double-glazed glass wall around the cheese room. The bakery ovens were outside our house covered in tarpaulins, the mixer was in a storage unit, the house was jampacked.

'It was all right after that quake – it's not so good now after the June 13 quake, but back then there was no liquefaction, the drive was straight as a die, the Food Safety Authority didn't close us down, we had Riccarton Farmers' Market and people could phone us up any time of the week and come and buy cheese from our garage. And we were building this place using all the materials from the old shop.'

Their staff managed to find work about the city.

'Tash, who is our main baker, did some work with Lizzie de Lambert, Lisa found work with Tonto at Vivace … somehow they

all hung on.'

In January Canterbury Cheesemongers reopened in premises at the Arts Centre that were bigger and better lit than before, and trade was brisk, until February 22. A dull day. They were having an unusual lull.

'There was no one in the shop when it hit. We'd had one or two jolts when there were customers in and the place does rock about: it was built in two parts – the bottom in the 1950s and the top in the '60s and they move differently. So that day it rocked a lot but we all managed to get out. The stone eaves of the Arts Centre were crashing down, and everything was smashing down and full of dust. It was a horrible event.'

The new walls of their shop were cracked but repairable. A greater problem was that although it was green-stickered and could be entered, it lay within the CBD Red Zone, a no-go area that included all the badly damaged buildings around the Arts Centre and an art deco apartment block across the road, St Elmo Courts, which was in a dangerous state.

Like many business people in the central city, Martin wanted to get into his building, but the rules were strictly enforced.

'You could have a business in the city and ask for access and they'd just say, "Tough!" But the Arts Centre had its own architects and assessors and when I rang the manager he said, "Look, I'll get you a yellow hat and a yellow jacket and you can come and inspect with us." Officially, we weren't allowed back until about a month later, but during that month I came in umpteen times with the Arts Centre crew and rescued all the hard cheeses.'

Another offer of help from within the industry was invaluable.

'The people from Karikaas out at Loburn rang up and asked if we wanted to store our

cheese out there. They had big cheese rooms. We lost all the soft cheeses, but we managed for about six weeks to store all the hard cheeses there.'

On April 18, after St Elmo Courts had been demolished, Montreal Street was rezoned and Canterbury Cheesemongers reopened.

'It was much quieter this time. And we have been less busy ever since.'

The little yellow van has been pressed back into service.

'Back in February, when we were so busy here, we had stopped doing the market and were going to take the van back to the people in Fairlie. But we'd been delayed and so the van was still here in the city. Lucky again!'

They were able to buy back the van and since then they have continued with the Riccarton Farmers' Market. They were also able to retain their staff, with the assistance

'The stone eaves of the Arts Centre were crashing down, and everything was smashing down and full of dust.'

of the government subsidy and business interruption insurance, which they had taken out in January.

'Our agent said, "You'll never need this but take it anyway." We were closed for eight weeks but they were able to come back when we reopened and they've been with us ever since.'

As we've been talking there has been a steady stream of customers: a couple of work-men in hard hats popping in for coffee and filled rolls, some Australian tourists pausing on a walk around the central city. Sarah has fielded an enquiry from a restaurant on the Coromandel for a stilton. A woman – a psychotherapist who grows vegetables as a sideline in a few poly-tunnels at Gebbies Pass – has arrived carrying bags of salad greens to add to the cabinet with its pottles of buffalo mozzarella from Clevedon Valley and

Philippa Morse's duck-liver mousse.

It's time for Martin to get back to work. On the morning of that first quake in September, I remember walking down Salisbury Street past the Cheesemongers. Martin and Sarah were standing with others outside their shop, masonry from the building next door littering the pavement. There were tears, shock on every face, such evident distress.

It has been tough. An appallingly worry-ing and difficult year. When he recalls that morning, Martin pauses. He looks away at the piles of stone around the Arts Centre, the wire fences, the carpark that used to house the little booths of the Saturday market. For just a second his expression is sombre. Then he takes a deep breath. He smiles. He has a wonderful engaging smile.

'Yes,' he says. 'We've been lucky. Luck, all the way.'

'*The neighbours were leaving, but cars were getting stuck. Unless you had a 4WD you weren't going anywhere.*'

They just don't get it, people outside the region: being here, in the thick of it, has been tough.'

Natalaya Pitama is most definitely 'in the thick of it'. She lives and works in Kaiapoi, a small township 19km from Christchurch that has seen some of the most devastating quake damage in the entire region. About 30 per cent of housing will be demolished and will not be rebuilt. It is a time of deep stress: like many others, Natalaya and her immediate family are all zoned red and will need to move. Raised here, the descendant of generations who have made this area their home, she is doing her utmost to make this painful transition more tolerable. She works as Kaitoko Whanau, employed to assist local people through the convoluted and difficult process of abrupt change and adjustment.

What this means on a daily basis is getting her three-year-old son, Zion, ready each morning to go to pre-school or to his toua, who lives only eight houses away. Her husband, Diccon, heads off to his job with a company in Woolston that specialises in fireworks: spectacular indoor and outdoor events. In 2012 he will start a new job at the Lyttelton port.

Natalya works from an office in Kaiapoi that is shared with the Waimakariri Earth-quake Support Service, Waimakariri Council and the Darnley Club, which provides care for the elderly in the district. It's known locally as 'the blue building' (it's painted blue) and most people know what and where it is. It's hard to miss. At any time there can be from five to 25 people working there: more if there has been an announcement from government or local government about the region.

'We can have people in paying their rates, or journalists preparing stories, or

government ministers in the office. People are in and out all the time, so it can get pretty busy. We're all working closely together, and although I'm seconded from another agency we have formed a team. You can't do this work without the support of colleagues.'

Natalya's professional qualifications are in social work, but this year her energies are focused on practical problems associated with the earthquake.

'Helping clients with the process – the insurers, the lawyers, understanding the jargon, getting their houses built, going through project managers, understanding the implications of being under or over $10,000 or $100,000 worth of damage, sorting out the options, whether they want to stay in Kaiapoi or in the district. Sometimes it's helping out with kai, or petrol, or how to get from A to B.'

It's hard for Natalya, too, seeing people

move away and knowing that they won't ever be coming back. She was raised here, though actually born 11km away in Rangiora. 'But I usually just say I'm from Kaiapoi. All this area has centuries of great proud history. This is where my bones are. Ko Tuahuriri me Arowhenua ka hapu: Tuahuriri and Arow-henua – down Temuka way – are my hapu.'

Her parents moved when Natalaya was one, to the house on Feldwick Drive where they have lived for the past 38 years.

'That was the only home I knew. Feldwick Drive. We all grew up there. There were seven of us, and I was the middle child. Everyone around us on that side of Kaiapoi went to school at Kaiapoi North. It was the type of community where you didn't know street numbers: you just knew that that was the Pitamas' house, that house was so-and-so's. Our house was a Maori Affairs place. There were quite a few of them built back

in the '60s and '70s around the east side of Kaiapoi. Those people, most of them, still live in those houses. And most of them are going to have to vacate them because they have been red-zoned.'

Natalya grew up among friends, playing tennis on the road as we all did back when roads were quieter places, riding their bikes on the riverbank and being told to 'just be home by dark'.

'You still knew the people you went to kindy with. It was a close community and it was good, being all together.'

In September 2010 she was working as a youth worker in the district.

'I got the job in 2008. I was pregnant at the time but I didn't know I was. Zion was a bit of a surprise. I took maternity leave and after being at home for one year with Zion I went back to work and my husband stayed home for a year. In 2010 he went

back to work too and Zion stayed with his toua three days a week. We each worked four days a week. We had a routine. We were just humming along.'

Holidays were spent down in Dunedin, visiting Diccon's parents, or over at Lake Hawea at a family crib. No worries.

'We were renters but that didn't bother us. The important thing was that we were all together and had time with our baby. We felt like we'd worked it out pretty well.'

And then …

'I remember Diccon saying, "Get out of bed!" He was going for Baby in his cot, who slept right through it. I just remember trying to get to the doorway and saying, "We need to get out! The house is going to fall on us!" But Diccon was saying, "No, this is the safest place." Then I was thinking, "I've accepted that I'm going to die but please, let it be a blow to the back of the head. That way it'll

be nice and quick." I became calm after that.'

When it finished, the adrenalin was rushing. Natalya wanted only to get out, to get away, aware that the Kaiapoi River was only a couple of blocks away. Outside they could hear cars starting and the voices of neighbours gathered on the street. Everyone was talking. Mud had oozed up everywhere – their house was still standing but their yard was filled with water and sewage.

'It was yukky. So I wrapped our boy up, packed some clothes but – you know what? We had no petrol: two cars, no petrol. So we couldn't move. The neighbours were leaving, but you could see water coming down the

road. Cars were getting stuck. Unless you had a 4WD you weren't going anywhere. There's one corner where the pipes were huckery – really shocking, mate. The sewers were so old and cracked they can't be repaired. It would cost millions.'

They tried to walk to Natalya's mother's house but the mud and water were deep and they didn't have gumboots. Since escape was impossible, they went back to bed, but not to sleep. In the morning the sightseers began arriving.

'People with cameras while people were digging themselves out. I wasn't in the frame of mind to dig. I just wanted to get out, to

'*When you look at a map of the areas affected it's a mighty chunk.*'

take my baby boy and leave. Make sure he didn't die.'

She saw her mother walking past with her dog.

'She said she was going down to New World for milk and bread! I didn't know that New World was severely damaged at the time, but I said, "Mum! We've had an earthquake!" She said, "Someone said you can walk along the riverbank." I said, "Mum, there *is* no riverbank!" '

The river had not flooded but its banks had suffered. Somehow, later that morning, Natalya and Diccon managed to drive out to Woodend to fill up with petrol and supplies. When they returned, Natalya did not want to stay in the house that night. No sewerage, no water, no power. Across town, on firmer ground, Natalya's aunt's place still had services so they moved over to stay the night with her.

'The town was completely divided. The east side, Golden Grove, behind the Maori Dam, Courtney Downs – was pretty much hammered. Pines Beach and Kairaki were in the same boat. Some people in the city thought it was just a few streets, but when you look at a map of the areas affected it's a mighty chunk.'

The damage, however, was not evenly spread. The zoning put in place since the quakes does not necessarily reflect the state of individual homes and land.

'My sister is in a red zone in Kaiapoi but her house is pretty much intact. There's no visible land damage where she is, but it's been decided that it's just not economical to restore services, so she's going to have to leave anyway. It's pretty shocking.'

Faced with liquefaction and aftershocks the family decided to leave, arriving in Dunedin the day after the quake looking 'the

'Diccon saw this old lady blowing a kiss at one of the boys in a digger. He said it was very cute.'

worst Diccon's family had ever seen us. We hadn't slept the night before. The shakes were still hefty. We just drove straight through. The traffic was heavy. Everyone was getting out.'

The marae at Tuahiwi and others around the country were taking in people.

'They gave them bedding, a meal, everything. It was very cool. One of the things about Maori is we know how to deal with large numbers of people. I mean, we know how to co-ordinate a crowd. I'm so proud of what they did.'

Meanwhile, Natalya's brother had arrived from up north to help dig away the liquefied silt around their mother's house. Facebook had become the main source of communication and another brother in Australia was able to go online and contact others who also came around to help. At the end of the week Natalya and her family returned home.

'I was the only driver in the family at the time so I did all the driving around here. It took ages because of the police blocks. They were checking to make sure only residents went through but they were always stopping me: "Who are these people?" "My mum, my sister …" Every time!'

Help flowed in from all corners.

'Friends, family, volunteers, churches, businesses, water trucks that arrived to water the road and keep the dust town, neighbours, people we'd never spoken to. The smiles, and the "How ya doing?" This kaka brings out the best in people. I loved it.'

Power had been restored, and portaloos appeared on the roadsides. There were crews everywhere working on the roads, including crews from elsewhere in the country.

'We were all really grateful. Diccon saw this old lady blowing a kiss at one of the boys in a digger. He said it was very cute. We had

180   THE QUAKE YEAR

a crew just outside here, fixing the water, and it must have been a pain for them having to stop every time we went out. They were so patient.'

As the aftershocks continued, damage became more pronounced. A neighbour's house was cracked right around at windowsill height. Their own house had not been badly damaged to begin with, but over weeks, minor cracks grew to metre-long crevices, foundations sank, the floor developed bumps and 'the golf ball test proved we were going down'.

Everything was grey. On a windy day dust covered the town. It was, says Natalya, like a ghost-town. 'You'd go out to the front gate just to check that you were still there. When there were people visiting, sightseeing, taking pictures, at least you knew you still existed. But when they left, well … we felt alone. A ghost-town …'

Despite reassurances that September had been 'the big one', Natalya was not convinced.

'I just knew there'd be more.'

A centre – the Recovery Assistance Centre, known as 'The Rac' – had been established in Kaiapoi to help local people with the process of repair.

'Someone called and asked if I'd be interested in working with Maori in the North Canterbury area. So I began work as Kaitoko Whanau for this region. People came in or I went round, helping wherever I could. It's not so much general social work as specialised earthquake work. But you pick up all the emotional and physical stuff along the way.'

She was impressed at the speed with which the Waimakariri District Council sprang into action and felt that really, at that level, 'we were well looked after'.

At the end of the year, just before

Christmas, Natalya and her family went to Palmerston North.

'Thank you, Palmerston North, you rock! Like many other places around the country, Palmy had people go up for some time out. My whole family were booked into the Coachman Inn. The staff and everyone looked after us and so many others with openness and hospitality. We were so grateful, and we slept so well!'

The Boxing Day quake made little further physical impact in Kaiapoi – though Zion, who was in the bath at the time, noticed the water slopping and for the first time mentioned the event he now called 'the shakey-shake'. By February the shakey-shake was becoming an event of the past. The rebuilding of Kaiapoi was under way.

'February 22. You wouldn't believe it … We had a meeting that day with the council. They were going through the whole process: what zoning colours we'd have, how the remediation would work, we'd been given clusters of streets we'd work with. The week before we'd gone out to check on our cluster in the Waimak Red Zone. Everything was co-ordinated. Everything was ready to go. We were going to go out and let everyone know exactly what was going to happen and how we could support them with temporary accom- modation during the rebuild. From 9am to 12 on February 22 that's where we were.'

At 12.51pm Natalya was driving down Marshlands Road, on her way to another meeting in Aranui.

'I was driving and thinking that I'd stop at the Palms for a feed. Then the whole road went up and down. At first I thought, "That's a hefty wind!" I stopped. I couldn't drive. Later my brother-in-law in Denmark said, "How long did that quake last for?" And I said, "It didn't stop!" It just kept on

rumbling.' I had the radio on and my first instinct was to ring the office on Pages Road to say sorry, I'm going to be late. Then the second one hit and I heard on the radio that there had been multiple deaths.'

She returned to Kaiapoi, picked up her son from her mother's place, then drove out of town.

'I just drove. Headed north. My husband was in Christchurch – pretty much at the epicentre. I turned back after getting as far as Waikuku. I thought I'd be able to get petrol but everywhere there were queues, so I went home again. Diccon got back about the same time as me. The mayor and the community board and council members were driving around checking on people. They called in and said, "How are you going, Natalya?" And I said, "Fine." I wasn't.'

A friend had been killed. He had been helping a woman at the Asian Food Court and was struck on the back of the head.

Natalya pauses. Tears in her eyes.

'I remember sitting here years ago, moaning about a cabbage tree that was outside Mum and Dad's house. It was such a pain in the arse, leaves stuck in the mower when you were doing the lawns, and I was saying, "We need to cut it down, get rid of it." And this friend said, "You don't cut those down!" I said, "Why not?" And he said, "You don't cut those down. They're markers. It's marking where you are." He said, "It marks where the Pitama are." Now every time I see that cabbage tree I think of that. When they knock the house on Feldwick down I'm determined they'll leave that cabbage tree so that it marks where we were.'

February changed everything.

Kaiapoi was not physically affected as badly as other areas in the city, and Natalya and her colleagues moved over to help at the

recovery centre in more drastically damaged Brighton. But psychologically there had been a profound change.

'We thought we were invincible. But in February, people died. We weren't invincible at all. And this was just so vast.'

Change also occurred at the bureaucratic level. Responsibility for recovery passed from the hands of the local council to the larger government body, CERA. Under their leadership, the future is taking shape.

So, what would Natalya like to see happen in Kaiapoi?

'I'd like for everybody to have a place: land set aside that is safe for everyone to build on and live on, rather than people making money out of all this. In my head this is not what this was about. There are hardly any rental properties in Kaiapoi and the rents are massive. People are moving back into homes that are unstable because they don't have anywhere else to go. I've visited houses that no one should be living in. What I want most now is for people to have some control over their lives again, because they haven't for over

*'When they knock the house down
I'm determined they'll leave that
cabbage tree so that it marks
where we were.'*

a year. Their lives have been in the hands of
nature and of other people.'

For Natalya, moving away is not an
option.

'People say, "Oh, you're renters. You can
just go wherever you like. The world's your
oyster!" Well, I'm sorry, but no: Kaiapoi's my
oyster. I don't want to go anywhere else. I
don't think people understand that.'

So she does whatever she can to give
people some control in all this. And personally, she tries to make sure that her own
family have fun.

'We do nice things with Zion; we've got
annual passes to the Antarctic Centre, and
Willowbank. This Christmas my brothers are

coming back home for a last Christmas at my
mum's, on Feldwick.'

In the long term Natalya believes Kaiapoi
will move closer to Woodend, that the land
on which her home stands will be remedi-
ated, and that eventually a future developer
will come in and put houses there again. But
in the interim the 'east side' will have gone.
That area by the Kaiapoi River.

'It's the river,' says Natalya. 'We were
defined by the river.'

And a new marker has joined the older
markers in this landscape. When people say
where they come from they no longer say
they come from 'the east side'.

They say they come from 'the red zone'.

NATALYA PITAMA

185

'Who cares if the grass is long? It's so irrelevant.'

Patsy Turner

We talk one sunny afternoon on the lawn next to the Akaroa Museum. Daisies are thick on the grass. It is quiet. The summer rush has not begun. Only a few tourists wander along Rue Lavaud, popping in to see the diorama with its display of pounamu, the whaling kettle, the antique French dolls, and the special exhibition of electrical appliances – kettles, a washing machine, a stove, an iron – gathered from around the peninsula to commemorate the arrival of electricity back in 1911. Patsy is slender, with lively hazel eyes and long lustrous hair she wears in various ways: plaited, loose, pinned up in a knot. Today it's a single braid. She rolls a cigarette and we begin to talk.

Yes, of course she remembers the September quake. She was in her cottage in Pipers Valley, fast asleep when she was shaken from her bed. She leapt, barefoot, to the doorway as suitcases stored on the top of wardrobes flew about the room and a large mirror fell and shattered. Nothing to be done but brace.

'It was like,' she says, 'being on an old ship in a big storm.'

As soon as the storm calmed her son Nik rang. Her cellphone was by the bed. Not her torch, of course. Nor a pair of shoes handily placed by the doorway.

'We didn't do things like that then, did we?' she says.

But somehow in bare feet she picked her way through the broken glass to the phone. Nik in his flat in the city was okay, while out at Pipers Valley a good portion of his vast collection of Transformers – a thousand at least – had hit the floor with a deafening crash: constructed of sturdy plastic and naturally being in possession of superpowers, none was broken. Patsy texted her partner Andrew, who was staying at his mother's. She spoke

to her parents in the city who were also safe. Then she decided to go back to bed. It was cold. It was dark. It seemed the sensible thing to do. Her cat Neil climbed in too. When it was light, she got up and dressed. For some reason she cannot fathom, she presumed she would be going to work as usual, until her boss, Lynda, texted to say that the museum would be closed.

'That's when I decided,' says Patsy, 'that I wanted boiled eggs. I don't know why, but I really *really* wanted boiled eggs. So I lit a fire – no power of course – to boil water. I hadn't noticed the chimney was cracked, but fortunately I didn't set fire to the house.' In fact the house, built of heart timber assembled with mortice and tenon in the 1850s, withstood the quake remarkably well, sturdy on its totara piles.

That night neighbours – 'Marilyn and Jack – very resourceful people' – invited 'a

little refugee gathering' of residents in the valley to a communal meal cooked on their woodburner.

'It was nice, not being alone. That was the hardest thing: being alone in the house and not knowing what was happening. My brain felt scrambled. It took ages for instance before I figured out that I could listen to the radio in my car.'

Over the next few days the car also became useful for its heater. Friends arrived and pointed out the scorch marks on the wood around the brick chimney-breast. Cooking eggs on the open fire was most definitely not going to be good idea. They helped her take the chimney down and from then on, for almost a year while she waited for the quake bureaucracy to approve and install a woodburner, her only source of warmth inside the little cottage would be an electric bar heater. She stuffed a mattress into

the ruined fireplace to keep out the draught. The car was a cosier option.

The museum reopened and Patsy returned to work. She noticed that it was easy to spot visitors who had been through the quake. There were the tourists who had been shaken from their hotel beds in the city. 'There was this American, a big guy, from the ice.' (Akaroa is a popular destination for Americans returning from the base in Antarctica, especially in September/October at the end of a winter deployment.) 'He just couldn't stop shaking. He was on the point of crying, just a mess. And there were Christchurch families who had come over to get away from the city. You could pick them too. They looked ashen.'

She remained wary, too, despite assurances that the hundreds of aftershocks were 'releasing energy' and therefore reducing the risk of another 'big one'.

'I just wasn't convinced,' she says. 'I knew there'd be more.'

In February she was in Christchurch for a hairdresser's appointment.

'Andrew's mother gives me one every year – highlights, the works, as a Christmas present. At midday I was at Ginger Meggs in Ballantynes. It always feels a bit surreal anyway, coming in from this little cottage with chickens and mud to the city and all those racks of lovely clothing and sophisticated people gliding around in the Contemporary Lounge. They'd hung up my coat but I'd kept my bag, because it had my cellphone and I was meeting Mum for lunch. Thank god for that, because I'd never have got it back. So I was sitting there at this long central table with my glossy magazine and my cup of coffee and the colourist had got almost halfway round with all these foils. And then it started to shake.'

To begin with she hung on to her cup of

coffee, but then the shaking grew in intensity and there was clearly no point in that.

'It was definitely "Give up on the cup of coffee!" We all just jumped under the table, all the people sitting on either side and the hairdressers – but it had a glass top and that started sliding around and my colourist took the initiative. She said, "Grab your bag!" and took my hand and we scrambled out.'

The scene in Ballantynes had become more surreal.

'All those beautiful clothes I'd walked past only half an hour before were lying on the floor and there was dirty water spewing all over them from breaks in the ceiling, a complete contrast. We got out somehow onto Colombo Street when there was another shake – a 5.7, a big one. I think that was when the cathedral spire went. I think it was there when we first got out. The noise was incredible. There was almost a pause though before it started: a kind of suspended moment, then the alarms started – car alarms, shop alarms; the buses screeched to a halt, people started moving, screaming. I had my bag so the first thing I did was dial Nik and he was okay, and then I could begin to think.

'The hairdressers were amazing. They were worried about my hair – that the foils had to be removed before the bleach damaged it, or, as one of them said, "It'd definitely be a layered look next time!" I didn't care about my hair but they were making sure we were okay. I mean, they could have run for their lives but they didn't: they asked us which direction we were walking in, so that no one was on their own. Some of them had huge journeys ahead of them, like out to Sumner. There were four of us heading north toward Bealey Ave. So I set off with the colourist, Charlotte – we were holding hands, we just couldn't let each other go. I had on these

'It was that, or pinot noir.'

stupid little sandals but we took hands and ran under the overpass that crosses Colombo. There were people saying, "Don't come under here. It'll fall!" But we just hung on to each other and ran.'

Progress was slow. A thick white fog covered everything. Grit glued itself to skin and hair and tasted of lime mortar. They picked their way through rubble to the Square. Her brain, Patsy says, was working very slowly. She saw no one trapped or bleeding. A man pushing a bike said, 'Oh my god, the cathedral's gone.' Andrew rang to say he was in his car on Bealey Ave. Liquefaction bubbled up in geysers. The bridge across the Avon was cracked, but they held hands and walked on. The memory is physical, imprinted like the disjointed and vivid memories of childbirth.

And along the way Charlotte looked for water to rinse Patsy's hair. Nothing was possible. Liquefaction bubbled on all sides but it

was thick and claggy. The river ran milky and inaccessible beneath a broken bridge with cracked and buckled banks. The fountains in Victoria Square had emptied. When they eventually reached Bealey Ave they found Andrew in his car jammed amidst six lanes of traffic, crammed bumper to bumper. There, Charlotte and Patsy parted company: Charlotte carried on to find her grandparents in St Albans while Patsy and Andrew inched to her parents' place in Merivale where Patsy was finally able to rinse her hair. No water in the taps, but a half-filled Pump bottle in the kitchen.

'It was that,' says Patsy, 'or pinot noir.'

They drank the wine instead. Patsy's brother and his family were already packed into the car and ready to leave that afternoon for safer ground further north. Andrew headed off to find petrol, a quest that took him all the way out to Rangiora and round to

Belfast where he found a functioning gas station that took cash only. He and Patsy finally returned to Akaroa late that evening. The old mill cottage in Pipers Valley had sustained little further damage.

And what are her thoughts now, a year after the first quake hit and everything changed? Does she have any observations to share? She thinks for a minute. Then she mentions her butterflies.

'I couldn't help noticing my caterpillars,' she says. She breeds monarchs and native red and yellow admirals in her garden. The admirals are endangered at present, the numbers dwindling hugely before the onslaught of a predator wasp introduced a few years ago to control white butterfly in the vineyards. It has turned its attention instead to other butterflies, including these big beautiful velvet-winged creatures. Clouds of them hover round special sanctuaries like her garden. In autumn, dozens feast on the blackboy peaches that ripen and fall from the tree at her back door.

'I plant swan plant and let the onga onga grow. The caterpillars live on the leaves. The admirals fold the leaves over themselves while they pupate.'

The caterpillars are banded with gold. She saw how they hung on the leaves after the quake, still munching.

'They weren't disturbed at all. All they were thinking about was what leaf to eat next. Sometimes I think having a complex brain isn't such an advantage after all.'

She wrote a haiku to celebrate the butterflies' resilience:

> *after the earthquake*
> *caterpillar eats*
> *the next leaf*

Blessed however with a complex brain, Patsy is less sanguine. It's hard to relax now.

She places her clothes where she can find them before retiring for the night, feels a little flicker of caution when climbing into the bath, pushes plates and glasses well back on the bench, and has taken down from the walls anything that might break. She makes sure she always has petrol in the car, sufficient tobacco, a few bottles of wine. She no longer bothers about mowing lawns.

'Who cares if the grass is long? It's so irrelevant.'

She is living instead for the moment because you don't know what might happen next. She has always professed to believe in living for the moment – but now she truly lives that way. Life is a 'continuous series of "nows".' That is a reality. The only thing that matters are family, friends, relationships. She worries for the people who are so much more affected than she has been: the people with families in the city, the children in particular.

She rarely travels herself from Akaroa into the city (the local expression is 'going over the hill', for the journey involves climbing up and over the Hilltop before reaching the plains on which the city lies.)

She did, however, 'go over the hill' once. Two months after the February quake she went into the city to complete her hair appointment. The salon had moved to a veterinary clinic near the airport. She was seated as before, and Charlotte had begun winding foils into her hair.

'I was so pleased to see her. We talked and talked. I think we'll be friends now, for life.'

Suddenly another client leaned across the table.

'I remember you!' she said. 'Last time we met was under a table on Colombo Street.'

They talked too: Patsy and Val, who comes from Sheffield. And she too, says Patsy, will be a friend for life.

What has happened to him personally is of far less importance than what has happened to the city as a whole.

John Wilson

John Wilson works from home, in an old villa in Woolston that he shares with his partner, Ashley. The tree-lined banks of the Heathcote lie at the end of the street. The garden around the villa is leafy and casts a soft shade on the front-room study where John works, writing books and articles on New Zealand's history and architecture. For 20 years he was editor of the quarterly magazine of the Historic Places Trust. His publications include architectural guides and rural histories, most recently an account of Akaroa's little brick powerhouse and early experiments with electrical genera-tion. His study is lined with maps, photos of mountains and shelves laden with books. More bookshelves occupy walls in the living room, containing books about Peru, London, American Indian history, Frank Lloyd Wright, Mark Twain. Art and architecture predominate, for this has been a lifetime preoccupation: buildings, and in particular the buildings of Christchurch, the city where John has lived with a few interruptions for over 60 years.

When I ask him about the quakes, he says that they were not for him especially disastrous.

'I never felt personally in danger, in either September or February, and this house got through all right. I mean, I certainly felt the force of the quakes: we were up at Arthur's Pass in February and the bach shook back and forth. You could tell from the direction of the shocks that if it was bad there, it was certainly going to be really bad back in Christchurch. But it was never frightening. The bad thing for me is what has happened since.'

What has happened to him personally is of far less importance than what has hap-pened to the city as a whole.

To Christchurch.

Of course he has experienced some personal loss. All sorts of things that once made living in the city satisfying and enjoyable are no longer possible: pleasant weekend bike rides, for example – to the library, along the riverbank past the suburbs of Edwardian villas and through the stone and brick-built streets of the city centre with their idiosyncratic ornamented frontages and architectural detail. But the personal loss is as nothing compared with the general loss the city has endured.

'The city I've known all my life – since my family moved here in 1951 from Timaru when my father became the minister at Knox Presbyterian Church – has simply disappeared.'

John has lived in many other cities in a long and busy career: St Louis, Boston (where he was a graduate student at Harvard, writing a PhD on Chinese history), London,

the ancient stone city of Cuzco in Peru, Geneva …

'There has always been a funny sense that Christchurch isn't a great city compared to those cities. But Christchurch is my hometown. It's the place I know, it's where I grew up. You always accepted its deficiencies and shortcomings – in architectural terms, I mean – because this was the place that you were familiar with, the place that you loved.'

But now hundreds of the city's buildings have been summarily demolished or are listed for imminent demolition: the Press building, the Fisher building, the Venetian Gothic McKenzie and Willis building, the Oxford Terrace Baptist Church, the 1930s Baptist Church in Beckenham, the Stone Chamber of the Provincial Council Buildings, the former Canterbury Public Library, the Woolston Library, St Luke's and St John's, the Carlton Hotel and Knox Church on

their opposing corners, the two cathedrals, Anglican and Catholic. The list goes on and on.

'I'm left wondering,' says the architectural historian, 'what do I think of Christchurch? What exactly holds me here?'

There is a residual loyalty to the city that demands he not turn his back or abandon it, but the city itself is simply not the place he knew and loved for so long. He describes a strongly visceral connection with the city's built landscape that found expression first back in the mid-1970s when he returned from the US to work at the *Press* as a leader writer.

'I was, by modern standards, grotesquely underemployed. All I had to do was produce a single leader every two or three days so I had a lot of time to do other things.'

He had returned in 1974 from Boston, with its beautiful and highly valued 18th- and 19th-century central-city landscape of dignified brick residential terraces and revered civic buildings. He recalls the impression made on him by Harvard's buildings, Commonwealth Avenue, Boston's new City Hall and Trinity Church.

'When I got back here I used to go upstairs in the Press building to the archive and look through copies of the old illustrated *Weekly Press*, and that was when I recognised that this place too had its own interesting heritage of buildings. It was actually quite remarkable for its concentration of styles, all contained in such a small area. The buildings were small and exactly to scale. They weren't necessarily classically proportioned, but they were perfect.'

He began writing feature articles – 'dozens of them' – about Christchurch's architecture, particularly when individual buildings became news, generally because they were threatened

with demolition. In 1984 these articles formed the nucleus of a book, *Lost Christchurch*.

He is clear about its original purpose.

'It was a propaganda book, saying, "This is the record of what we have lost." People were patting themselves on the back and congratulating themselves on what had been preserved, but I was saying, "Wait a minute: look at what we've lost! Stop pulling these buildings down. Start thinking about them seriously and start looking after them!" It was quite ironic, really, because between 1984 and 1987 the buildings came tumbling down like ninepins.'

The book may not have achieved its author's purpose but it did find a wide audience, selling out its first print run almost immediately and going into reprint: 4500 copies sold in all. The book with its photographs of grand houses and theatres, mercantile buildings and civic structures, is now a collector's piece, something to look out for in the antiquarian booksellers.

By the time of its publication John was employed as editor of the Historic Places Trust journal and involved in various heritage battles up and down the country, though Christchurch was always personally his primary focus.

'I got so angry with local body politicians who had the power to preserve significant buildings but failed to act.'

There were successes. He cites the old public library – which this very morning, by one of those ironies of timing, is coming under the wrecker's ball. I passed it on my way here to Woolston. Gaping holes punctured its upper floors, its pediments and ornament were already a pile of rubble behind protective cordons on the road. John mentions also the Government Build-ings in the Square, which were saved from

demolition in the 1990s and might yet be preserved following the quake. And he mentions the Coachman Hotel on Gloucester Street, which came within five minutes of being demolished in 1994. Others were less fortunate: the imposing Masonic Lodge and the Synagogue on Gloucester Street both came down.

In 2010 John was embarked on a thorough updating of *Lost Christchurch*, adding a long list of more recent losses to the sorry roll-call of demolition. By September he had almost finished the project. In 45 seconds, however, all that changed. Now the rewritten book is expanding by the day.

'Writing it has become my therapy in a way,' he says. 'And it is now a very different book. It's no longer polemical, arguing the case for conservation. It is more of a lament.'

In the first few months after the September quake the city lost as many of its noteworthy old buildings as it had lost in

the previous half-century. Between 1960 and 2010 the catalogue of the city's notable Victorian and Edwardian buildings was reduced by about half. Since September that remaining half has dwindled to about a tenth.

And, in John's opinion, a huge number have been demolished unnecessarily.

He has not of course been able to visit the buildings himself, for they are cordoned from public scrutiny. But from a close examination of photos he can see no reason why many could not have been repaired.

'The Press building, for instance: that could have been rebuilt; the little Fisher building on High Street corner; any number of others need not have been demolished, but the insurers, the owners, the council didn't want to be bothered. There wasn't the will. In Italy, when Assisi was hit by two earthquakes and six months of aftershocks in 1997, all sorts of old stone buildings associated with

St Francis were ruined: the basilica, churches, chapels, pilgrims' houses. But within three years they had been restored, stone by stone. Whereas here, Gerry Brownlee's immediate reaction within hours of the quake was that he planned to 'pull the old dungas down' – despite the fact that most of the deaths in the quake were caused by two modern concrete structures. As arguments Brownlee and his team have used a) public safety, and b) "We've got to get the CBD up and running!" But all those old masonry buildings were relatively small and could have been cordoned off and left a year or two while plans were drawn up, and combined public and private funding was put together.'

Such an approach, he fully understands, would have been difficult and time-consuming. Above all, it would have required willpower. And that simply wasn't there.

'I've felt completely impotent in the face

of this massive indifference,' says John. After decades spent defending the aesthetics of a city he feels he has no option but to disengage. There is no point, he says, aware of the irony of the expression, in beating his head against a brick wall.

'I take my hat off to those who can muster up the energy to keep fighting. Anna Crighton, Ian and Lynne Lochhead, Ross and Lorraine Gray, Brendon Burns are still writing letters to the paper, fighting, and I have huge admiration for them, but personally I just feel numb. I can't find the energy even to write letters. The forces ranged against preservation are simply too overpowering.'

He cites the list of 40 'heritage buildings' drawn up by Iconic, a group of heritage activists and property owners convened by Brendon Burns in the immediate aftermath of the February quake. The list named buildings the group thought should be repaired

and saved. That list, he says, is already down to 10. And really, it does not address the central issue: saving this building or that will not mean that the city's built heritage has been preserved. It is much wider than that. He quotes his local precinct in Woolston.

'There were four major heritage buildings here: the former Woolston Post Office, the nugget factory, the Woolston library and the building that became the Holy Smoke café and smokehouse. Plus some others. Of them all, only the Holy Smoke building has survived and that's because it was strengthened a few years ago when it changed use to become a café. It will remain, but now it lacks its context. There'll be no other evidence of its place as part of the old communal life of a Christchurch working-class suburb. It'll be this solitary old brick building in a sea of concrete block and tilt slab.'

So what would John have done, had he

possessed the powers of a government minister charged with saving heritage buildings in the aftermath of this year's quakes?

'I would immediately have placed protection orders on certain buildings and insisted that they were not to be torn down until all the options had been explored. Instead, especially after February, every impediment to pulling down listed buildings was instantly removed. I would have used the political clout that this government has but refuses to exercise, to say to insurers and owners that this building or that is listed and cannot be demolished, and if you need public assistance, come to us and we'll talk about it. It could have been done, but it's too late now. Most of it's gone.'

Now, he avoids the central city. On the day they returned to Christchurch after the February quake he recalls driving down Brougham Street and seeing the Sydenham Community Church, a building of great historic and architectural interest, reduced to rubble. His heart, he says, sank at the sight. The first time he passed the ruins of the former Provincial Chambers he came close to tears. In December, cycling up Ferry Road towards town, he halted at the traffic lights on Barbadoes Street. He looked left and saw a digger crunching its way through the former convent that in recent years had been home to the Christchurch Music School. The convent chapel – a marvellous gem with its soaring arched ceiling – was already gone. He had been hoping against hope that it might have been saved. When he looked away to avoid witnessing the destruction of another building he had loved, it was to see the empty sites of the former Anglican convent and, further north, of the Provincial Hotel. Could he bear to stay in Christchurch, he wondered, as the city of brick and stone he had loved

'The city I've known all my life has simply disappeared.'

became a phantom, fading city that existed only in his head?

What has been lost is not merely brick and mortar. A building, he says, has an almost spiritual aspect, retaining all that has occurred within its walls. It's not an easy concept to express.

'It came home to me years and years ago in the *Te Maori* exhibition. The criteria for including an artefact in the exhibition were not always the aesthetic criteria that the museum curators valued. The Maori articulated very clearly at that time that for them an object became a taonga because it had been handled and possessed and used by the ancestors. Aesthetically it might be inferior to another object but it had that quality. That's what I mean when I'm talking about "authentic buildings".'

Reconstructions will not therefore be adequate to recover the past. He uses as an example Knox Church, a place he grew to know very well as the minister's son back in the 1950s. Its walls have fallen away, leaving the bare bones of a wooden arch: that, he feels, should be retained, made visible, as the building's authentic frame.

But really, the city has gone and there is no option but grief. Piecemeal redevelopment, the complete lack of visionary leadership, 'dinky' plans for light rail between city centre and university, the brutal pragmatism of engineers fixated on clearing the decks to make way for something new, the bizarre continuation of work on an unnecessary extension to the southern motorway when whole suburbs exist with potholes and diversions – they all rouse in him furious anger.

Buildings matter deeply to him. They have always have had a strong emotional impact.

'I remember in 1974 going into the Town Hall for the first time and thinking, "This is a great building." And from longer ago I remember the Banking Chamber of the old National Bank and going in there with my dad when I was a child. He was quite a commanding man, but in that building with all its grandeur and its impressive presence he was temporarily diminished. I also remember going to the Civic Theatre with my mum to orchestral concerts and how exciting it was for a young lad being in that building among the crowd going up the stairs.'

When those buildings went, the memories associated with them became harder to retain. The post-earthquake demolitions have left him feeling adrift, the anchors to memories cut.

He recalls also a moment when he stood in the beautiful Gothic hall of the old Provincial Chambers. He was about to address some meeting for the defence of one of Christchurch's buildings. He looked around and was overcome by the awareness of all the others who had stood before him in just this place and spoken: FitzGerald, Moorhouse, Rolleston …

'Why do we bother?' he asked his audience on that occasion. 'Well, we look up and around at this building, and the question itself disappears.'

Photo information

Unless otherwise specified on this page, all photographs in this book were taken by Juliet Nicholas.

CHRIS MOORE: Press building photographs courtesy of Fairfax New Zealand.

KAREN DUNCAN: The photo of the toppled Rolleston statue is courtesy of Fairfax New Zealand. The Christchurch City Council enabled access to photograph the head of the statue in storage. The two photos of a Christchurch Public Hospital operating theatre on pp. 36 and 37 taken by Karen Duncan.

AMY GREGORY AND JAMES ALLEN: The wedding photo courtesy of Jenna Bellis.

SALLY BLUNDELL: The photo on page 66 is from *Norse Gods and Giants* by Ingri and Edgar Parin d'Aulaire. The artwork on pp. 72–73 is *I seem to have temporarily lost my sense of humour* by Wayne Youle and is part of the Christchurch Art Gallery Outer Space Project.

BEV PROUT AND QUENTIN WILSON: The historical photos on pp. 76–79 courtesy of Bev Prout.

HELEN WEBBY: The portion of musical score reproduced on page 94 is copyright Chris Cree Brown. The photo on page 99 courtesy of the Canterbury Symphony Orchestra.

SIENE DE VRIES: The woodcut of *Kellers Peak* (referred to in text as Panama Rock) on page 107 is by Saskia van Voorn.

JAIMINI SHURETY: The photo on page 115 courtesy of Fairfax New Zealand.

JENNY GLUE: The photo of the Repertory Theatre at night courtesy of Repertory Theatre.

MARTIN ASPINWALL: The poster image on page 169 is courtesy of the Love Christchurch campaign for the Canterbury Development Corporation (CDC).

JOHN WILSON: The 'before' shots of the Provincial Chambers building (pp. 196 and 205) and the old library building (page 204) are by Duncan Shaw-Brown. The Knox Church image on page 200 (black and white) was supplied by John Wilson.